KANSA
OF WILLIAM STAFFORD

2ND Edition

Edited by Denise Low

Commentary by Thomas Fox Averill, Kirsten Bosnak, Robert Day, Steven Hind, Jonathan Holden, Caryn Mirriam-Goldberg, Denise Low, Al Ortolani, Linda Rodriguez, Ralph Salisbury, William Sheldon, Kim Stafford, Robert Stewart, Ingrid Wendt and Fred Whitehead

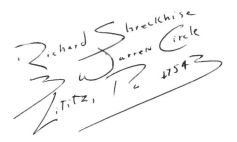

WOODLEY MEMORIAL PRESS
Washburn University

ISBN 978-0-9817334-6-3
Library of Congress Control Number: 2010925068

Woodley Memorial Press
Washburn University
Topeka, Kansas 66621

http://www.washburn.edu/reference/woodley-press/

1990 ACKNOWLEDGEMENTS OF POEMS

The following poems by William Stafford are reprinted (with permission of Graywolf Press from *Smoke's Way: Poems from Limited Editions 1968-1981*, ©1983 by William Stafford: "A Walk with My Father When I Was Eight," "Inland Murmur," "North of Liberal," "Even Now," "Happy in Sunlight," "Temporary Facts," "Time Capsule," "The Girl Who Died, Who Lived," "On Her Slate at School," "A Farewell Picture," "A Gift for Kit."

The following poems are reprinted (with permission of David R. Godine) from *Segues: A Correspondence of Poetry,* with Marvin Bell, © 1983 by William Stafford: "It Still Happens Now," "Key of C – An Interlude for Marvin," "How My Mother Carried on Her Argument with the World."

This poem is reprinted (with permission of *Poetry* © 1974): "Oak"

The following poems are reprinted (with permission of Harper & Row) from *Stories That Could Be True: New and Collected Poems*, © 1977 by William Stafford: "The Peters Family," "One Home."

First publication for these poems by William Stafford were in the following publications: "Roadside Markers for West of Dodge," "Living on the Plains" in *Ark River Review*; "At First National, "Out Through a Church Window," "American Gothic," "Fox Escapes Park Zoo," "All the Time," "Biography," "In the Old House," "Be Calm. God Has Offered Us Pretty Names," "Through Nature to Eternity," "Extension," "The Center," "Afterward," and "The Deaf Gardener" in *Cottonwood Review*; "Good Room," and "Willows" in *Kansas Quarterly*; "Coronado Heights," "Old Ways, New Ways," "A Briefing for Visitors to Our Planet" in *Little Balkans Review*; "Looking Back on the Weaving Room" in *New Letters*; "Because of the Rain" in *Pembroke Magazine*; "Home Economics" in *South and West*; "For a Distant Friend" in *Road Apple Review*; "The 1940's" in *The Soft Press*; "An Early Massacre" in *Sumac*; "A Dream" in *The Phoenix*; "Graduate" in *Quixote*; "Lake Wendoka" in *Thistle*; "In a Country Cemetery" in *The Hudson Review*; "In Touch's Kingdom" in *The Southwest Review*.

2010 PUBLISHERS' NOTE

The Bob Woodley Memorial Press was established in 1980 by Robert Lawson with a mission to publish Kansas authors. Current and longtime Woodley President Larry McGurn acknowledges the press as "the only literary press in the nation devoted to Kansas themes and Kansas authors." Indeed. Though we initially published predominantly poetry collections, now, in our thirtieth year, we have published over forty books by authors with a Kansas connection in fiction, creative non-fiction, and poetry.

Not surprisingly, William Stafford is the most renowned and respected poet with Kansas connections that Woodley Press has had the honor of publishing. In celebration of our tenth anniversary, Woodley published Mr. Stafford's collection of poems entitled *Kansas Poems of William Stafford,* suggested and edited by acclaimed Kansas poet in her own right, Denise Low. Also, not surprisingly, this small volume has been sold out and reprinted multiple times, and we continue to get requests for it from individuals and institutions of higher learning on a regular basis. It is for this reason that in celebration of Woodley Press's thirtieth successful year as a non-profit small press run by volunteer writers, we are proud to present *Kansas Poems of William Stafford, 2nd edition*, again edited by Kansas poet and now former Kansas Poet Laureate Low. This volume includes the original Stafford poems, plus additional essays on the man and his work by current notable writers who have been inspired by William Stafford and by Kansas alike.

---K.L. Barron & Dennis Etzel Jr.,
Managing Editors of Woodley Press, 2010

4

1990 PUBLISHER'S NOTE

The Bob Woodley Memorial Press, established to publish Kansas writers, has existed for ten years now, having published, on average, two paperback volumes each year. To celebrate this longevity, encouraging to a non-profit small press dependent on volunteer labor, Denise Low suggested a collection of William Stafford's Kansas poems. Since William Stafford is certainly the most celebrated of Kansas poets, and, while resident and poet laureate of Oregon, frequently returns to Kansas for readings and workshops, everyone on our board knows him and his work quite well. We were all enthusiastic. Mr. Stafford generously agreed to this collection and Denise Low, a distinguished Kansas poet in her own right, agreed to edit it. This is that book: celebrating the tenth anniversary of The Woodley Press, and encouraging Kansas poets everywhere to persevere.

--Robert Lawson, Editor-in-chief, Woodley Press, 1990

1990 INTRODUCTION

By Denise Low

The poet William Stafford is easy to like. He holds out his hand to new readers, urging them to "Love the earth like a mole" and to "each day nuzzle your way" ("Starting with Little Things"). The poems in this collection—mostly connected to Stafford's Kansas origins—offer a vision of brotherly affection for the earth and its creatures.

Likeable, yes, but these are not naïve, primitive paintings. The poems are subtle, dark, godly, and paradoxical at once. Stephan Stepanchev calls them poems of "existential loneliness and Western space." They are not stereotyped rural landscapes of barns and wind vanes.

Although the Midwest and Kansas place names occur throughout Stafford's books, he is not a regionalist. He lived in Oregon most of his career, but he is not an Oregonian writer, either. His imaginative process goes beyond facile description of place. Stafford himself asserts his aspirations:

> I wrote about Kansas, I wrote about Illinois, I wrote about Indiana; wherever I was. And if I moved tomorrow I'd write about where I showed up, no matter where it was. And so my attitude is this: where you live is not crucial, but how you feel about where you live is crucial . . . .

So the Kansas of these and many other Stafford poems is not a geographic locale, but something more profound, something made more complex by human imagination: "I can say without any problem that the language is what I live in when I write."

The familiar scenery in these poems—the town of Liberal, the Cimarron River, the "Midwest Home"—are surface traces of deep-set human intricacies. More happens than a scan of horizon:

> You glance around. The world
> has turned into now:
> at a bluff on the north bank
> forty years ago someone
> did not come to meet you. ("North of Liberal")

Here a geographic space is elaborated by the variables of time. According to physicist Fred Young, if time is held constant, space

6

goes to infinity; when space is held constant, time moves to infinity. Stafford works the tension between the two, in order to transcend both, as he explains: "Working back and forth between experience and thought, writers have more than space and time can offer. They have the whole unexplored realm of human vision."

Further, the timeless Kansas plains suggest a mystical dimension. In high school the young poet camped overnight by the Cimarron River and experienced a "dream vision," which he describes: "No person was anywhere, nothing, just space, the solid earth. . . . That encounter with the size and serenity of the earth and its neighbors in the sky has never left me." This serenity still informs Stafford's work.

Judith Kitchen points out a "fixed vision" throughout his years of writing, a "central, unchanging sensibility." She further notes that "there is often an attempt to duplicate, at least in feeling, that original dream vision." The parallel of sky and horizon-line to a vision of spiritual unity contributes to a verse of magnitudes. Hometown memories, the landscape, family relationships, and animal life are seen in the context of Stafford's larger quest.

Within this created domain, language is re-formed. The vocabulary is selective, as noted by Jonathan Holden:

Such words as "deep," "dark," "cold," "God," "home," "near," and "far" Stafford consciously uses as a symbolic shorthand, as components in that set of interlocking metaphors which defines his vision of the world.

Stafford's intention reveals itself, obliquely, in "many words associated with the Quaker faith" (Kitchen), such as "witness" and "friend." Description is spare, elliptical, and often abstract in all his works. His texts shape a style as distinctive as a handprint. Syntax, too, is rearranged. The poet inverts phrases and transposes nouns into active verbs ("Under my hat I custom you intricate, Ella"). Cryptic omissions and compressions occur. A mole's paws become "spades, but pink and loving: they/break rock, nudge giants aside/affable plow" ("Starting with Little Things"). This "mole," much like the poet himself, demands mental agility of the reader. The verse creates a new vocabulary of thought, which requires time and patience, much like friendship.

Stafford writes guidebooks about learning a territory well. He illuminates the universality inherent in detailed moments and landscapes. And despite cruelties that border this created land, seen in the poems "Even Now" and "At First National," still it is an ordered world. Every person's story has dignity, and when a stranger approaches on your side of the sidewalk, proper etiquette is to smile and say "hello." After all, he might offer conversation like these poems.

Holden, Jonathan. *The Mark to Turn: A Reading of William Stafford's Poetry*. Lawrence: University of Kansas press, 1976.

Kitchen, Judith. *Understanding William Stafford*. Columbia: University of South Carolina Press, 1989.

Stafford, William. *Kansas Poems of William Stafford*. Topeka: Woodley Press, 1990.

-----. *The Way It Is: New and Selected Poems*. St. Paul: Graywolf: 1998.

-----. *Writing the Australian Crawl: Views on the Writer's Vocation*. Ann Arbor: University of Michigan Press, 1978.

Stepanchev, Stephen. *American Poetry Since 1945: A Critical Survey*. New York: Harper & Row, 1965.

CONTENTS

9

11

I. THE LAND WOULD HOLD US UP

CORONADO HEIGHTS

Where we touch the rock, a little cold shiver
begins: this is the place where Coronado
found that cities of gold are dust,
that the world had led him north beyond
civilization, beyond what was good.

And right down onto this prairie grass
he fell. His helmet tumbled right here.

He smelled the earth and felt the sun
begin to be his friend: he had found
a treasure, the richest city of all.

Wheatfields frame this place today,
a gift: how the riches of Mexico,
the wandering tribes, the golden wind,
all come true for us, bowing
in reverence with Coronado.

15

INLAND MURMUR

In the Cimarron Hills
on the sod no plowshare knew
pigeons tumbled through the air
and on the grassblades there
the rain fell in the dark
and the wind blew.

On the Cimarron Rock
the crooked water broke
a splash and then a swirl
from arid gorges gritted full
far in the softest curve
of the Cimarron Hills.

On the swell of earth
or in the swirling flood, I knew
tumbling clear the pigeon feel
and the rain touch as the wind blew
over the curve the world was of
in the Cimarron Hills.

Plowshare air, the dark wind blew.
Water broke, a swirl softest curve.
Swell of earth curve the world.
    Come come so they.

[Inland Murmur]

NORTH OF LIBERAL

You open your mouth to say, "Wait!"
then falter: far away,
the open the winter, and
the four of you crunching snow
along the Cimarron.

That path is still there; it led
miles and miles into brown country
so far that to go there again
makes a new turn, almost makes
your life another person's.

You glance around. The world
has turned into now:
at a bluff on the north bank
forty years ago someone
did not come to meet you.

Crunching snow, Cimarron...
miles into brown country.
■ new Turn, the world.
 Forty years To meet you.

North of Liberal

17

A GIFT FOR KIT

Fence wire sang—spring wind—
where I stood among tumbleweeds, ready
to wander, too, by Willow Creek.

Listen—it was only the world
adrift in the days, and a sound
of the sky singing to it,

Where friends of mine once lived,
and I came there to understand: it was like
seeing and knowing amid what you see.

A meadowlark brought me back,
just flying its road and singing,
being alive. I brought home this tumbleweed.

THE PETERS FAMILY

At the end of their ragged field
a new field began:
miles told the sunset that Kansas
would hardly ever end,
and that beyond the Cimarron crossing
and after the row-crop land
a lake would surprise the country
and sag with a million birds.

You couldn't analyze those people—
a no-pattern had happened to them:
Their field opened and opened,
level, and more, then forever,
never crossed. Their world went everywhere.

ONE HOME

Mine was a Midwest home—you can keep your world.
Plain black hats rode the thoughts that made our code.
We sang hymns in the house; the roof was near God.

The light bulb that hung in the pantry made a wan light,
but we could read by it the names of preserves—
outside, the buffalo grass, and the wind in the night.

A wildcat spring at Grandpa on the Fourth of July
when he was cutting plum bushes for fuel,
before Indians pulled the West over the edge of the sky.

To anyone who looked at us we said, "My friend";
liking the cut of a thought, we could say, "Hello."
(But plain black hats rode the thoughts that made our code.)

The sun was over our town; it was like a blade.
Kicking cottonwood leaves we ran toward storms.
Wherever we looked the land would hold us up.

Made our code, sang hymns.
Buffalo grass, wildcat spring
Grandpa, Indians pulled the West
Black hats leaves we ran
     land would hold...

One Home

20

EVEN NOW

Wherever I go such winter shakes our town
that I look at the ground and feel the storm
      that shudders to get in.
Wherever I go, it's night there; weather
buffets at the stores while people listen—
listen: furious echoes batter the roof
      and rattle the tin.

Wherever I go the whole world's air
Caught in a river rushes the door to bend and pound
hinges that strain and whine out a myth:
"Here's where it all could start again;
again, wanderer—
      now! Turn round!"

Wherever I go, whoever I become,
that Christmas weather wheels through streets
      and the alleys behind,
and—remote and secure though I thought
      to have been—
for thousands of nights a tin sign has flapped,
flapped a message I can't quite read,
      caught in such wind.

WiNTer shakes grouhd FuFions echoes
World's air - whine a Myth: TurN ronud.
    ChrisTmas Message
    Christmas Message

21

ROADSIDE MARKERS
FOR WEST OF DODGE

1. A Scene for Future History

Here, in the latter days, there will be
fields, a hayrake, a storm, and no one
at work. There will be years like this:
something gray walking the fields,
iron rusting away, a strange light
beginning to descend on the shiny weeds.

This place belongs to the sky.
It will be wilderness again.

2. You've Seen It from Lake Cheyenne

There is a groove in the grass
where the biggest clouds pass
dragging their shadows across,
finding the line to follow exiles.

It goes where those people went,
a train of them, unweary, no end,
hunting the fabled land—
those years. . . these years. . . on. . . .

1.) A Scene For Futnre History

Latter days Fields a hayralle, be years
like This; irnnrusting belongs To the
sky. wilderness.

2.) you'se seen iF From Lalle Cheyenne

groove The biggest clouds Shadow's across,-
People went a train those years. Thess years ... on --

3) Reminder Stone

Journey you are oN look dowN;
this place? It May here. 22

3. Reminder Stone

All who pass, pause:
from a source inside
we hunt the goal.

This journey you are on—
how far? Look down:
this place?

It may be here.

*Roadside Markers
For West of Dodge !!*

VOCATION

This dream that the world is having about itself
includes a trace on the plains of the Oregon trail,
a groove in the grass my father showed us all
one day while meadowlarks were trying to tell
something better about to happen.

I dreamed the trace to the mountains, over the hills,
and there a girl who belonged wherever she was.
But then my mother called us back to the car:
She was afraid; she always blamed the place,
the time, anything my father planned.

Now both of my parents, the long line through the plain,
the meadowlarks, the sky, the world's whole dream
remain, and I hear him say while I stand between the two,
helpless, both of them part of me:
"Your job is to find what the world is trying to be."

Trace on the plains a groove my father
To happen wherer she was mother called.
Blamed the place my fatheer planned.
Meadowlarks, sky, world's whole dream
between the two helpless part of me.
    "is trying to be"

Vacation

24

HAPPY IN SUNLIGHT

Maybe it's out by Glass Butte some
time in late fall, and sage owns the whole
world. Even the obsidian chips
left by the Indians glitter, out of
their years. Last night's eager stars
are somewhere, back of the sky.

Nothing where you are says, "It's me
only." No matter how still the day,
a fence wire hums for whatever there is,
even if no one is there. And sometimes
for luck, by neglecting to succeed that day,
you're there, no one else, and the fence wire sings.

The obsidian chips Indians glitter,
    eager stars back of the sky.
Nothing where you, a fence wire hums,
    if No one is there, sometimes for luck;
        No one else.

[Happy In Sunlight]

25

FOR A DISTANT FRIEND

Where Western towns end nobody cares,
finished things thrown around,
prairie grass into old cars, a lost race
reported by tumbleweed.

And hints for us all stand there, small
or shadowed. You can watch
the land by the hour, what hawks overlook,
little things, grain of sand.

But when the right hour steps over the hills
all the sage flashes at once,
a gesture for miles to reach every friend:
Yes. Though there's wind in the world.

Things thrown, into old cars Tumbleweed.
Hints stand There, you can watch,
haws overlook, sand over the hills
yes— There's wind.

For A Distant Friend

AT THE BREAKS NEAR THE RIVER

Autumn some year will discover again
that gesture of the flattened grass, wild
on the Cimarron hills when a storm
out of northern New Mexico raided
Cheyenne country to hunt for rusty armor
left by Coronado, and my father sifting his
fingers in that loose ground of the Indian
campsite said, "Oh, Bill, to know
everything! Look—the whole world is alive,
waving together toward history!"

CEREMONY

On the third finger of my left hand
under the bank of the Ninnescah
a muskrat whirled and bit to the bone.
The mangled hand made the water red.

That was something the ocean would remember:
I saw me in the current flowing through the land,
rolling, touching roots, the world incarnadined,
and the river richer by a kind of marriage.

While in the woods an owl started quavering
with drops like tears I raised my arm.
Under the bank a muskrat was trembling
with meaning my hand would wear forever.

In that river my blood flowed.

Ninnescah amnskrat the bone water red.
Rolling, Tonching roots woods an owl,
like Tears, Under the bank Meaning —
Blood Flowed.

Ceremony

LISTENING

My father could hear a little animal step,
or a moth in the dark against the screen,
and every far sound called the listening out
into places where the rest of us had never been.

More spoke to him from the soft wild night
than came to our porch for us on the wind;
we would watch him look up and his face goes keen
till the walls of the world flared, widened.

My father heard so much that we still stand
inviting the quiet by turning the face,
waiting for a time when something in the night
will touch us too from that other place.

A little animal dark against the screen,
had never been, soft vild Night, the
wind; watch, him the nigthe walls.
My Father still stand, quiet waiting
For a Time that other place.

[Listening]

29

II. BACK HOME

FROM TOMBSTONES BACK HOME

1.
God said come in. I came.
Then God said get out.

2.
Vini Vidi Abscondi

3.
I never had a clue.

4.
I'm here.

5.
What's the hurry?

6.
I've gone to find my real name.

7.
Bad brakes.

8.
They called me Smiley.

9.
Sometimes I looked at the sky.

KEY OF C—
AN INTERLUDE FOR MARVIN

Sometime nothing has happened. We are home
at the beginning of summer. Somebody begins
to breathe chords on a harmonica.
"Why don't we tell how our lives will be?"
Sarah says—"I'll start: when I finish
college I'll move East and work in
a bank. In a robbery there a stray bullet
will kill me." Tom quits playing the harmonica:
"I'll work in Dad's drugstore. My wife and child
will die in a fire when the child is three."
He goes on breathing slow notes. Mary
leans back in the porch swing: "I'll marry Tom
and oh I'll hold the little one so close."
"I see exactly," Steve says: "After The War
I'll come back here and you'll all be gone. I don't
want to tell the rest." They turn to me:
"I'll live carefully, and a long time.
Years from now when I'm writing to a friend
I'll tell him what we said today
and how it all came true." –And oh Marvin,
even this part I'm telling you.

TEMPORARY FACTS

That look you had, Agnes, was a temporary fact.
Probably by now Time has it back.
From spiral nebulae I call it here now.

Through the trance of high school you pass along the hall.
Lockers clang the hours; you pass windows.
A Christmas candle shines on your hair.

On spellbound evenings you call your brother home,
coming toward the streetlight through shadows of the elm.
Shadows touch your mouth when you say a name.

All of these things were temporary facts.
Only for an instant Time gives them back.
In spiral nebulae a shadow goes on.

Agnes has it back, spiral nednlae ...
You pass windows, Brother home,
Touch your mouth, say a name.
Time gives then back shadow goes on.

(Temporary Facts)

TIME CAPSULE

That year the news
was a storm, a wind that
puzzled monuments. Wrecks piled up
on the Coast, and at year's end
after the party and song we sang
our old composition called "Friend,"
wrapped up the scraps for the stock;
then one by one
through perspective we took up coat
and hat and
were gone,
westward up the river
where flood-mangled cottonwoods
imitated grotesquely Governor
and President and Saint, bend by
bend, all the way home.

That year the news was
not only free, it was mandatory.
The barometer said "War."
To the west gulls came
in like tracers.

Back on the farm it was calm,
and pigs ate the greasy newspapers.

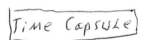

Was a storm, Wrecks piled up - song we sang
we took up coat and had flood, mangled
cottouwoods All the way home. the barometer -
"War." like Tracers. Back ou the Farm it
was carm and it seems
being calm it
wonderfounder

Time Capsule)

LOOKING BACK
ON THE WEAVING ROOM

It will be the days and the sound of the sewing
machine, the jays on the mossy trunks outside—
you know, like blue threads on every tenth tree.

It will be the gradually accumulating pattern of
scraps on the rug, and the benches creaking, and not enough
black on the shuttle to finish and beaters and then a long silence
to think, until the next shuttle pass, all slim
like a fish under the span of warp.

It will be each one taking a part of the weave
home, and then on. You can always get back,
just by the way you lean over a loom
and then look up and it's there again all around you,
    and Mary Jo making the tea.

Sound of The sen ing, jay's like blue
Benches cnches creaking shutte
To Finish, shctte pass, all slin,
of warp. It will be each. You cay always,
    over a loom aroud you, To !!

Looking back on The
Weaving Room I

37

AN EARLY MASSACRE

Backward on the wagon,
across the hopscotch, into
the shrubbery, we
carried the dolls.

Russ and Sam didn't like
that party anyway.

It would be later the rest
would find everything scattered,
and the overturned wagon.

That night I thought I *sleep*
heard the screaming.

Backward, hopscotch, the dolls.
Don, do not party awaway.
The rest everything scattered,
overtuwing, overturued wagou?
Night sleep.

An Early Massacce

THE GIRL WHO DIED, WHO LIVED

Last night an old sound came by chance;
dust regained its honest place
the way it stopped when years ago
that little girl who died, who lived
across our street, was lying in the rain
we played in till the church bell rang.

Back then we thought the minutes came
one at a time; but in the sound
that came by chance all minutes leaped
at once and bore me down, remembering.
I stood a stranger chance had struck
Or bells had caught; I leaned on dust,

heard the storm bring the neighborhood
onto our porch that afternoon,
gathered for help, all talking at once,
trying to regain our quiet place
before the girl who lived had died.
Fingers in the rain still identify her face.

AT FIRST NATIONAL

Every morning when day
crosses the street a calendar
flips over in the bank.
Pennies pooch out
the vault and roll into someone
else's account, and from all
fields corn and wheat
flow to dribble the ledger
where machines peck "Amen"
over the crops.

Somewhere the dust meets
to discuss the manager—how
in December he
always tightens fences in Wyoming
and sends deep-footed snowmen
to stop all payments in Michigan.

Later it is the meeting
to forgive him again;
of course all animals except
a few dogs vote no,
but always at the spring meeting
the states melt and vote yes, yes,
yes, with all kinds of flowers.

OUT THROUGH A CHURCH WINDOW

Sunday means different: flowers tell church-goers
what all the rest of the week is for.

A light—only the daily sun—shines gloriously
purple and rose through a permanent story.

Neighbors transform under that light, shining
briefly on their way into their dark places.

A man and a woman sing stairs in the air:
the organ comes down slowly where the rest of us are.

Afterward people go about their lives
remembering all week what their lives are about:

How the daily sun darkens, even toward noon,
how we are living a story in all our homes, toward night.

AMERICAN GOTHIC

If we see better through tiny,
grim glasses, we like to wear
tiny, grim glasses.
Our parents willed us this
view. It's tundra? We love it.

We travel our kind of
Renaissance: barnfulls of hay,
whole voyages of corn, and
a book that flickers its
halo in the parlor.

Poverty plus confidence equals
pioneers. We never doubted.

FOX ESCAPES PARK ZOO

When the bears paced like bankers
and the monkeys moaned and worried about the weather,
the fox curled back in his corner among the coons,

Now and then opening one yellow eye
over this tail and letting the fools
stop or go by or fall into his pupil.

When fall came and the leaves piled
there in the corner of the den, he was gone,
sly, fooling the poor mayor and the worried aldermen.

CAPTIVE

Calmly through the bars observe
how correct a tiger is:
the striped fur blends with cages;
how the iron parallels
the paw freed by your—calmly!—eye;
and if it's a big one—coincide—
how the stripes become the bars:
tiger flesh rejoins a fawn's,
commitment to the cub he was
before a shadow caged his ribs;
how he glides by appropriateness
into jungles while you stand
outside his eyes, beyond his bars:
captor, witness, victim—calmed.

LAKE WENDOKA

Under the sidewalk lay an Indian village—
we knew our state held a buried scream:
one world that moved and then
another world. We walked on both
when we walked our town.

Father tapped a rock and glanced around:
"It is all right to picnic here—
think what **they** did to us Mound Builders."
He glanced at Mother's braids in the sun.
"Do right today, Kids." Do right today."

Bob and I, the careless ones, we ran ahead
where a hillside opened and they built the dam,
long blue water flowing prairie lake,
slow waves lapping, rock to bank to sand:
Arapaho, Kansa, Cheyenne, Cheyenne, Cheyenne.

IN A COUNTRY CEMETERY

Their last blanket, the wind, has
torn the whole winter down, now fumbles
frozen trees, and heads on south alone.

Oh stream that touched their life,
tense as a fence wire, wild:
God lived where you are from.

And He waits when you have gone.

The wind, down frozen Trees.
Stiem, a Fence, God liveg watis whew.

IN A COUNTRY cemerery

46

ALL THE TIME

We live in a town clocks hurt. They chase
the young through the streets and corner the old
at bay on porches. Their big hands conduct
crowds in stations; their little ones pinch
and slice at the wrists held out for them.

Our people are caught by many little threads,
all slowly tightened by being tangled
in clock wheels that cannot stop or wait.
Vibrating steps of the second hand make
the town shiver. Everyone winks and cringes.

What I like are visiting tribesmen who think
a clock is a big pie or cake, and those
little sparrows that sing as they ride the minute
hand, and those few open-faced citizens
who wave back their arms all directions at friends:

They don't care whether a clock has wheels,
or what time it is.

Clocks hurt wrists held out for them.
Caught by threads being Tangled.
of the second winks and cringes.
A clock little sparrows wave back.
don't care has, it is.

All the Time

47

IT STILL HAPPENS NOW

You make me walk my town, its terrible
streets that peel day after day for years
and fall into the sky, till I'm drowned
in time. Even if I shut my eyes the lilacs
come their tide, and Pauline's old house
honks by in a long, low, dying moan
as I fade for my life, wild for this safety
of now, far from the thousand hurts—
those friends moving there still,
fresh, open faces, long bodies leaning
after my last goodby, when war came, and
we left all that seething, and put the lid on.

We walk my Town, Fall iNTo The sky.
Shut and iNTo the shurt my eyes —
old house, dyiug moan For my life.
Far From The Thousaud hurts there sTill.
open Faces bodies leaniUg last
goodby war caMe, leFt all all That seething

It still HaPPeNs NoW

48

PRARIE TOWN

There was a river under First and Main;
the salt mines honeycombed farther down.
A wealth of sun and wind ever so strong
converged on that home town, long gone.

At the north edge there were the sand hills.
I used to stare for hours at prairie dogs,
which had their town, and folded their little paws
to stare beyond their fence where I was.

River rolling in secret, salt mines with care
holding your crystals and stillness, north prairie—
what kind of trip can I make, with what old friend,
ever to find a town so widely rich again?

Pioneers, for whom history was walking through dead grass,
and the main things that happened were miles and the time of
day—
you built that town, and I have let it pass.
Little folded paws, judge me: I came away.

III. AT THE FAMILY ALBUM

AT HER SLATE AT SCHOOL

On her slate at school my mother wrote "Winter."
When she ran home the weather erased it.
For all the pain my mother saw in the world,
over her face the snow has exploded its little flowers.

"This is the part of the year," she called to us,
"excluded from tree rings: children, remember!"
Around our house were such tall legends,
everything carved by winds and rivers.

Even today they care, the temporary winds,
the prevailing rivers; and a giant in disguise
still knocks at our chimney. For awhile, children,
the trees around us have those years in them.

HOW MY MOTHER CARRIED ON
HER ARGUMENT WITH THE WORLD

We would sit down, after a visitor had
gone (reassured by lavish agreeable responses
and strokings), and my mother would not hide from
me her great treasure of saved-up reflection
on the oddity, poverty, blundering of the
just-pampered person who had been soothed. I
learned how kind you have to be so as not to
let others know their truly desperate situation
("Don't let them know!")—they are **other**.

Big people huff up like a cat, fierce or
scared. You hurry over to say, "You are big,
huffed-up, fierce." You don't say "scared"—
you want to meet them where they are. Your
expression studies theirs and becomes whatever
they need. When you leave them you often say, "Scared."

Once, away from the sound of the highway, we walked into
silent Wyoming, a hawk riding a thermal, one
smooth hill drawing our world into the sky.
Side by side we angled the hill, treading tough short
grass, now and then choosing which way to
avoid an arroyo. Mostly the spacious landscape
allowed straight, air-free walking. She told me:

Let's consider describing geniuses the way we describe
popular figures: How tall was Einstein? Pascal? Napoleon?
Eve Curie? Thomas Aquinas? Dante? Mother Mary?
Mohammed?
How impressive was Plato? Confucius? Aristotle?
Gandhi? Descartes? Shakespeare? Keats? The Brontës?

She thought the aggressive were losers. They had to use
methods only the desperate would use. Their lives were
ruinous. Without even knowing it, they forfeited
the game before they got started. She studied them and
shook her head. But to tell them would hurt them without
curing their disability. To an extreme degree they had
that almost universal burden of being other.

How can you keep others from feeling the abrupt
fact that they are—don't say it to them—other?
You listen carefully, and never allow the hail
of their multiple little blunders—or the vast
arc of their wild misunderstandings—to register
in your unswerving, considerate gaze.

The one who appears hurt, I learned, could be
the one who is withholding hurt from the others;
and for those of us rich in this wide, mild
gaze, we'd be worse than the others if like them.
This was her way—to suffer, lose wide-eyed, and
practice the ultimate put-down of her secret **noblesse oblige**.

A WALK WITH MY FATHER
WHEN I WAS EIGHT

Here is a space for the way the day started:
(   ).
Here is a word for the sun: (   ).
I can't fill these blanks for sure any more:
that day we were both young.

He showed me the creek I thought people dug—
a wild thing, we found, wandering;
we saw clenched lovers—"two spooners," he said;—
so calm he tamed even that wind.

By rich people's farms (they owned the world
and up into the hills that held
a place in the sky) we sang for their cows,
and belonged there, tramping their fields.

In town by dusk we owned such a day
that other days lined out through school
and on out: I could find them and live every one,
after that walk through the fields.

Here is a space(   ) the sun: (   ) both young.
Wandering, "Two Spooners" that wind.
They owned the world, Into the hills in the sky.
    I could find them - every one.

A walk with my Father when I was eight.

A FAREWELL PICTURE

My eyes look their twinned corridor far,
focus for a while, then lose again that
year it snowed the picture of the world
And radio clocks learned war by heart all night.

My father nailed only game with his rifle.
People, no; only the game—until
that year mistakes came up his arm and
shattered our snowflake faith's integrity.

Steady as ever was, but never again
so clear, so eager to be blind—
I see again and again that great snowflake
smash on my father's face like a valentine.

year it snowed, radio cloks heart all night.
Game with his rifle. until that maarmistakes —
our snowflake, so eagear to be blind —
Great snowflake father's face like a valentine.

 [A Farewell PicTure]

BIOGRAPHY

Two days were walking down the street,
One bright, one dark, and both my birthday,
glowing for my head. (Dark is delight for
me. Both my parents are dead.) That street
was the one we lived on, years ago—that is,
   while they lived.

Two days left that place; after my birth
nobody saw two days together ever again,
my mother said; and my father said the same,
but they always liked both kinds and welcomed
dark and light; both glowed for their head,
   while they lived.

The house they knew has opened;
it stands at large in the hills; its
door is the rain; its window evening.
Today I bend for roof have shelter
when it's cold, but that great house
arches for all, everywhere, for them, too,
   while I live.

down the street, one bright, , after my birth,
saw two days, dark and light, door is the ,
Foot house for them ....

Biogrphy *(But a papy is mose love*
coming more!

58

LIVING ON THE PLAINS

That winter when this thought came—how the river
held still every midnight and flowed
backward a minute—we studied algebra
late in our room fixed up in the barn,
and I would feel the curved relation,
the rafters upside down, and the cows in their life
holding the earth round and ready
to meet itself again when morning came.

At breakfast while my mother stirred the cereal
she said, "You're studying too hard,"
and I would include her face and hands in my glance
and then look past my father's gaze as
he told again our great race through the stars
and how the world can't keep up with our dreams.

midnight and flowed up in the barn.
holding The earth morning.
"Studing Too hard", in my glanre—
Through The stars The world can't keep—
with our dreams!

Living On the plains!

59

HOME ECONOMICS

What came, our mother took: like rain,
barrels of it from off the eaves,
to wash our hair, the purest rinse;
and the swept-up dust—for the sweet pea trench,
the best mulch for the brightest flowers.
Wind worked the well;
sun bleached the clothes;
winter made real the holidays.

Troubles just made her rich, like this:
"A woman like me, to live so long."

GOOD ROOM

In our best room, only a kitchen,
we touch cloth—in towels—, touch
metal stove, wood cupboards.
You look down the bread board: scars
time never needs to overcome.

The easy refrigerator door closes like this:
"**Forgive**." Inside, a light goes to sleep
comfortably, friend of lettuce, admired
by the eggs; and the meditative motor
suggests winter, then pauses all night.

Our best room that gives life, alone with independent
spices, content just to be in their jars:
while we live may your way be ours.
May we never forget order, the various
world brought by recipes to man's taste—

The work of many men made into everyone's home.

IN THE OLD HOUSE

Inside our Victrola a tin voice, faint
but somehow both fragile and powerful, soared
and could be only Caruso, all the way from
Rome: I traced my fingers on the gold letters
and listened my way deeper and deeper:

Far people. There had been war; grownups
were brave about it, but they didn't really know.
Caruso was sorry so hard that our town
became part of the world. On the rug the Victrola
dug in and shook on its little carved paws.

THE 1940'S

In a mirror that saved those days
nothing is allowed to fall,
not even the way we used to be
that no one remembers now.
To that deep time I turn,
to you in the silver of then
all alone in that air
caught by the fastest lens
that makes an instant stand.

I look back toward you
down the long lonely room
only one breath wide
I had to travel through.

GRADUATE

An old anguish, real as a nail,
wakened me: did I ever make up
the neglect my college taught?

How kind we were to each other at home—
but home sank, yours and mine,
that year. It's gone.

Now I carry whatever the sun remembers,
and millions of little splinters lean
and make time go by.

Besides one's heroic acts, there are those
where you don't decide, where
morning comes, and you meet new things.

And the old ways die.

THINKING FOR BERKY

In the late night listening from bed
I have joined the ambulance or the patrol
screaming toward some drama, the kind of end
that Berky must have some day, if she isn't dead.

The wildest of all, her father and mother cruel,
farming out there beyond the old stone quarry
where highschool lovers parked their lurching cars,
Berky learned to love in that dark school.

Early her face was turned away from home
toward any hardworking place; but still her soul,
with terrible things to do, was alive, looking out
for the rescue that—surely, some day—would have to come.

Windiest nights, Berky, I have thought for you,
and no matter how lucky I've been I've touched wood.
There are things not solved in our town though tomorrow came:
There are things time passing can never make come true.

We live in an occupied country, misunderstood;
justice will take us millions of intricate moves.
Sirens will hunt down Berky, you survivors in your beds
living through the night, so far and good.

TIME'S EXILE

From all encounters vintages ensue,
bitter, flat, or redolent. When we met
sunflowers were in bloom.
They mark the highway into Kansas yet.

My unreal errands, once the sun goes down,
fade into streetlight shadows.
Extenuate as the bright lights will, they run
into the hometown shadows.

I'm alongside old happenings when they flare;
like the dog that found the wounded quail
that came up through breast-feather shadows
into the sights and set their wings and sailed

the proximate field, and melted with shot
into another field—I bring things back from everywhere.
I am a man who detours through the park,
a man like those we used to meet back there—

Whose father had a son,
who has a son,
who finds his way by sunflowers through the dark.

IV. NOT ONE LEAF GONE

WILLOWS

Every one
has to learn
humility.

Say they settle
on an island:
floods take them—

They have to swim,
a few stragglers,
to a bend

On the shore.
There against
the barbed wire

They have to stand
in cold light
and begin

To oppose
everything.
They become

Their own kind—
ancestors,
bent again

In slow relief,
their incredible
years-long ballet,

Lithe at first,
until they bow
—absolute—

All the way.

OLD WAYS, NEW WAYS

Some things it is odd to say, though
once you think about it they are
all right, like the upside down song
a bird sings, flying past, reflected in the water.

"Goodbye tomorrow," someone greets you—
that means "Hello" in the old language
used by thoughtful people, not the new way
of the rest of us after the bird flew over.

BE CALM. GOD HAS OFFERED US PRETTY NAMES

Let fawn autumn come,
no thin first ice before;
and fallen or almost, the leaf
again begin to coast earthward
beside that still face once more—

Let the whole earth wear
the wind, negligent, steady, wild,
to rummage, brush, lean forward,
then lose again forever
each moment's child—

Let summer go. Never
enough, let it wane.
"Always!" people call,
Then inexorably know
some lost, dear face, and the rain.

BECAUSE OF THE RAIN

Someone I touched because of
the rain surfaced last night.
We touched, then no one.

You know the world plans it:
a thin dress, and the cold,
a night turned into wind.

You know how things go.
And they have to—I know. But the rest
of the world turns away.

That person came back last night,
because of the rain.

THROUGH NATURE TO ETERNITY

1) A man taps a message out. A water pipe, say,
   leads through the ruins; on it he
   repeats, "We're here, we're here."

2) In cold early spring back home
   dogwoods in the dark firs would say,
   "Even if the sun doesn't come, we'll come."

3) An office in the clouds hears these things.
   They make a difference: a raindrop
   swerves, or on a hill a quieter boulder sleeps.

A DREAM

I scramble far to a niche
in the rock and look out:
the scorched earth.
I'll not cross that again.

Suddenly I know the world bathes
in invisible light, and the times
while we are in love wash
over and through all days, all nights.

Anything we do can fail—I
know that. In love, though,
there are millions of ways to fail:
all are sacred.

EXTENSION

Into the daylight I follow a blind man;
the sky is irrelevant.
I see the sunshine; I watch his hand,
how it moves looking for Heaven.

Be my sponsor, blind-man hand;
through touching let me learn
forward farther than ignorance
and backward more than has happened.

THE CENTER

Whenever you breathe God comes in:
"I'm home again. I'm home."
And curtains lean, then resume
their silent wait.

Listen—that sigh of welcome,
and after that no breath.
Wherever God stands, it is there that
the world will start again.

God comes in: I'm home their silent wait,
that no breath-sigh of welcome…
God stands, world with start again.

The CeNTeR

IN TOUCH'S KINGDOM

We use the stupid self:
a touch at a time are moved,
and we save each other—
from drift, from loss,
from Hell's deep gulf
that being alone could open.

We hold each other safe.
Refuse touch, you fall,
a loss too steep for thought,
too quick for light.
Hell has flames that leave you:
you go out.

Save each other From loss alone could opeu.
You Fall aloss Too steep - Hell has Flames that leave
yong yon out.

We Iouneh's Kingdom

AFTERWARD

In the day I sheltered on the sunny side
of big stones. In the whole world other things
were giddy: they moved. I leaned on the steady part.

Every day passed into darkness. Dawn
rescued the top of the rocks and the middle
and then me. The sun loved my face.

You can hardly believe what I did: when winter
came, when the nights began to be cold,
I dissolved away into the still part of the world.

Now it is cold and dark, and the long nights
return to the wilderness. One big rock is here
for my place. All else moves. I am learning to wait.

On the sunny side of big stones into darkness –
Top of the rocks. The sun loved my Fall.
The Nights began To be cosold, wilderness,
All ellelsmoves. I am learning to ~~whae~~ Wait.

[Afterward]

THE DEAF GARDENER

While he worked he was absent
some place the birds reminded him of.
He often stopped, almost threaded
or broken into by sound. It was the unexpected
almost brought him that sound.

Why should the deaf sing? He
liked others to sing, only that he could
put his hand where he could feel the print
of the notes, or taste cedar wood
like in Italy when smoke from shavings
meant violins in some old, old town.

Horked he was absent often stopped broken in to —
by shund. Him that saund. Deaf sing? He could —
Feel the print or taste cedar wood - violins —
in some old, old Town. (The deaf Gardener)

The Deaf Gardeuer!

79

OAK

When we heard the long wind coming home
we held the walls up with our hands.
One tree talked in the storm in our yard:
its leaves held on, too brown to fall,
shaken as the wind was long.

Today those thin leaves rustle again.
I heard a dead branch tap the blind.
I put my hand—the walls are gone,
but a tiny voice comes up my arm:
forty years. Not one leaf gone.

Heard the long walls up with our hands in leaves,
brown brown to Fall shaken as the wind. Branch tap
tap the walls are goum Forty years. Not one leaf gone.

V. WITH WILLIAM STAFFORD

APPROACH WITH CAUTION:
Introduction to *The Phoenix Papers*

By William Stafford

These writers launch their attempts, their conjectures, like flare above an unexplored continent. Fitfully lighted, that great unknown stretches out there around us.

And sometimes, flatfooted, we readers or hearers have to hold back, skeptical, wary: it is risky to commit to excursions beyond the immediate, the usual. Offered greatness, we lean away and wonder. We glance at each other out of a mist. Perched on our own little islands, blinkered from knowing, we live tamely at the edge of riches. Only occasionally do we glimpse possible landscapes that stagger the mind and the emotions.

For think of it—maybe our days dole out to us only little bits of what life could be. Like whoever it was who discovered America, we begin to boast. We think we inflate our reports: and meanwhile what is out there far surpasses any lie and "inflated" report. We can't catch up, even, with our wildest "lies."

Poetry assumes the license to cut loose. Not just into new forms but new sequences and angles that ordinary vision doesn't offer.

Phoenix Papers will show how lively a time this license can create, with springing surprises and hidden connections among feelings and ideas. These poets are urgent to take life and make more than life out of it. They put a spin on things; they are ready to give it a try, see what happens.

But to make claims for poetry … is to encounter possible rebellion, for some readers; and such rebellion can lead to doubt and unfriendliness, which can collapse poetry into something ridiculous. As Wordsworth remarks somewhere about the poet: "You must love him, 'ere to you/ He will seem worthy of your love." You have to lend attention and be ready to accompany the writer on excursions that can expand your visions and feelings.

Once you grant permission for exploration, you become available for a life that includes adventure. As one of the writers in this collection reminds us: "Buddhism flourishes where dragons are honored."

You are entering a world with strangeness in it. Please be open. Give a little. You may get back a lot.

February, 1993

Editors Note: This introduction was written for *The Phoenix Papers: 26 Lawrence Poets* (Lawrence: Penthe, 1994), edited by Stephen Addiss and Stanley Lombardo. However, this is its first publication.

AN INTERVIEW
WITH WILLIALM STAFFORD

By Steven Hind

*Steven Hind interviewed Stafford in Hutchinson, Kansas, on
February 6, 1984, while Stafford was a guest lecturer at
Hutchinson Community College. This interview originally
appeared in* Cottonwood, a publication of the University of
Kansas English Department *(Issue #34, Fall 1984).*

**As a point of departure, I was interested in whether there were
poets you caught fire from. How did your interest in poetry
start?**

STAFFORD: I've read many, many poets all my life. My parents
used to read to us, and they would read poets like Edgar Lee
Masters, Kipling, standard anthology things. The school poets, you
know, Longfellow and so on. And ... they had a gusto for all kinds
of books. Sometimes, I feel today that I prefer prose. I read more
prose than poetry in current writing, but I do read a lot of poetry.
When I get into a library, I go scuttling around, just the way you
eat olives at a party, you know, just nibbling all those little
magazines.

**I wondered about your parents and your interest in poetry.
Your parents seem to be such a powerful and unique force in
your work. I wonder if you think your growing up was
unusual for a Midwestern child.**

STAFFORD: Well, it wasn't until I met other writers later that I
thought it might be unusual. I thought this was the way everybody
was. But apparently not, because I keep meeting writers who felt
alienated from home, who were in rebellion against their parents.
Our parents were, I guess, unusual. At least . . . whether they were
unusual or not, I'll say how they are, or were. They were addicted

to reading. Not just in the abstract, but we'd just get out and walk to the library wherever we lived. Find the library, and start checking out books. And they read, not systematically or for any policy or educational value, but just because they couldn't help but read. They were helpless readers. (Smiling) And I caught it from them. I don't think I've met a young person these days who reads the way we read at home. Summer was an orgy of reading. The porch swing was where you would lie down in the morning and come in at night. (Chuckling) Or so I remember it.

This book we were talking about his morning, the Poulin *Contemporary American Poetry*, has a piece in the back, about you in which Poulin says that your work is a "highly personal poetry" but not "self-torturing nor confessional." (Stafford laughs.) Do you see your work as having escaped confession?

STAFFORD: I don't feel bad about confessionals. I want to start there. For instance, Robert Lowell interests me a lot, the poems about his background, confusions, bafflements, and so on. But, yes, I think my poetry has escaped confessional if that means accounts of suffering. I don't feel like a sufferer at all. I feel lucky, awfully lucky. I distinguish that from feeling deserving of good luck. I don't know about that. I put that out of my mind, but just that I have been lucky and happy, so it's not confessional in the sense that . . . well, I guess confessional implies something that you have to get rid of. But I don't feel like that in my poetry. It seems to me welcoming recollections rather than pushing away recollections.

I couldn't help but notice this morning when you read the poem—I can't recall the title right now, the poem about calling home . . . .

STAFFORD: Oh, yes, it's called "The Farm on the Great Plains."

Yes, I had the feeling that the poem somehow threw out a hook that caught you in a way that was very personally emotional.

STAFFORD: It's quite possible in a reading for this to happen to me—for me to be carried away by one of my poems. And in fact, I just keep some of my poems out of my readings, not because I don't feel all right about them, but because I'm not confident that I can go right through them with enough esthetic distance to make them effective. Actually, "The Farm on the Great Plains" is not quite in that category. I may have seemed to be caught up in it, and in a way I was, but not beyond controlling it for esthetic purposes. But there are poems like that. I had one in my pocket this morning, but I just decided not to read it. It's called "Remembering Brother Bob." It turned out that the family knew that poem. I didn't know whether they'd seen it or not. They said, "You should have read that poem." "Why didn't you read that?" one of them said. I sort of put them off, said I didn't know whether I could do it effectively or not.

Well, that was a wonderful performance of a poem, "The Farm on the Great Plains."

STAFFORD: That's fun to read, partly because it has dialogue, and I like that in anyone's poem, and partly because it tracks along toward something at the end, I think.

The issue of form and style comes up. I heard Marvin Bell talk about "the plain style on the plains." What about that in your own experience? Do you think style is something a poet can calculate or modify, or does it just come with the territory?

STAFFORD: Oh, that's good. That makes me stop. I don't have a . . . I ought to have a canned response to this kind of thing. But something in the way you say it makes me juggle a little bit in any preconceived ideas I had. For instance, I think style effectiveness comes through care. It can be chosen and cultivated by the individual. I don't want to deny this, but there is a part of me that says, yes, but for it to be ultimately valid, it must be arrived at by means of appetite. That is, if I were not available to the feelings of a certain poem, like "The Farm on the Great Plains," I would hate to try to concoct a poem like that because it might be wise to have one if you're from the plains. So it doesn't come to me as a result of calculation. It comes to me as a result of convergence between me and materials. But once it begins to come, I'm aware that it's coming, and I say welcome, welcome, keep on. If that makes sense.

Yes. I mentioned this morning reading Kathleen Norris writing about South Dakota and driving 400 miles to hear you, and you had said something to her about having her "on your radar." Do you have a sense of a literary community in the Northwest?

STAFFORD: I do have that sense. Probably, I'm sort of ridiculous to take this stance, but I would feel bad if I didn't register the blips where the writers are where I live. I think I know them. On the other hand, I know that some escape me. Some show up and they're doing something that I don't know about, but generally I have a sense of the presence of the people in an area who are writing, and a sense of what kind of writing they're doing. Very much so. Here, yes. So I read things like this new [issue of Cottonwood Press's] *Confluence,* and I sort of check again. Yep, blip, blip, blip. But then there are some I don't know, of course. Probably a majority I don't really know, their work, until I read through the book, and then they begin to register. And I like to do that. It's a matter of . . . like being able to find my way around a neighborhood.

That's a nice metaphor. You have spoken about the attention paid to poets in other cultures, other societies. I heard you speak about that in Dodge. Why do you think Americans in general aren't more interested in their poets?

STAFFORD: Well, I can think of several things to say about that. First I'd just latch onto that idea that other cultures pay attention to their poets. I've been astounded when I've gone to some lands where I could see rooms full of people who could repeat in unison poems of some poet, some poet I'd never heard of too, sometimes. So that's astounding. This is just a simple fact. Then, about America . . . well, I guess maybe the melting pot would be part of it. Our society is fractioned out among various peoples, and literary traditions. There just isn't a central tradition, so that I just don't think there's a voice that represents the groundswell of feeling and concurrence of ideas and traditions that there would be in some other cultures. That would be part of it. You know, this is partly German, partly French, partly English, partly black, and partly Indian. And if you can imagine a Black Elk having, not just a fractional part of the populace, but the whole populace, that would be like Ghalib in Urdu-speaking cultures. I mean that's one of my theories, which I didn't have before you asked that question. You think of maybe Langston Hughes, who can be appreciated by many people, but he can't, I guess . . . his central core of followers would be the first to agree that he can't be fully appreciated by those who don't share the culture. We just don't share the same culture.

You speculated that the very openness of our society might have something to do with it, whereas other cultures might appreciate things that had to be said by indirection.

STAFFORD: Oh, yeah. Yes, you can imagine the pressure. You can imagine the society in which there is pressure not to say certain things, but a need to say certain things, and someone comes along who can say them indirectly. That would give off a sharp whistle. (Laughter)

I'd like to ask some questions about poems in particular. There is a tone of a sort of enforced humility in your work sometimes, and yet you can be awfully tough about things that, it seems to me, you wish to criticize. As an example of that, I think of a poem called "Staring at Souvenirs of the West" that I saw in the _South Dakota Review_. You have Buffalo Bill staring "into his own gun barrel" and seeing "what his victim saw." You seem to banish the world of "Winchesters and war bonnets" in that poem, and the last scene is the death of Sitting Bull, his wife holding a cross "close in her hand when the shouting died." You seem to be suggesting there that we worship the wrong things as we consider the history of the West, that we glamorize the wrong people.

STAFFORD: I feel intensely revisionist about the history of the West. I'm not alone in this, of course, but the idea that through circumstances, through chance things and a kind of an out-of-control hero worship, we have become a nation that makes history of the West be John Wayne civilizing the West. It jars my sensibilities quite a bit, so it doesn't surprise me that it shows up. When you were saying that, I realized two things at once. One was .... The second thing really was, yes, in fact I do feel intensely critical or revisionist about the standard depiction of values in the West. The first thing, that's a little bit harder to get at, is my poems do have a kind of assumption of humility and non-corrosive flavor, usually, a kind of mildness even. The co-existence of those things is something I cherish. I want to be mollifying, but I do not want to be conforming. That is, I want to bring about a revolution in ways that will help the revolution to stick. I don't want to adopt the ways of the opposition to change the opposition. Well, I'm a pacifist. That'd be another way to put it. And most ways of revising or rebelling or bringing about a revolution are too much like what they are opposing. So I stare at souvenirs of the West, and my poems will often have what seems to me legitimately called coldness and deliberate causticness, sometimes. They're hard but, I hope, only where they have to be.

STARING AT SOUVENIRS OF THE WEST

What if a buffalo eye, big
as the wrongs done them, looked
into the lodges and hotels of Indians
and Whites? What if Buffalo Bill
stared into his own gun barrel and
saw what his victims saw?—if the mountains
came down to attend a memorial service
for their shaggy, mistreated citizens?

In parlors and lunchrooms let's have
crocheted work, and beads, a decorative bundle,
straw flowers, many sacred things
heaped over the guns and hard-eyed portraits these warriors
awarded themselves. Take your
Winchesters and war bonnets into that cold
you claimed, heroes. Here is a cross that
the wife of Sitting Bull hid: she held it
close in her hand when the shouting died.

South Dakota Review 18.4 (Winter 1981): 62

STAFFORD: I couldn't help thinking about, for instance, the wife of Sitting Bull. I think I wrote that when I was out at Cody, Wyoming, and saw the Buffalo Bill Museum. It's a pretty macho sort of worship that goes on there. Those gods are not my gods, that's all.

That's a nice introduction to another question. The title poem of your collection *Stories That Could Be True* creates this possibility of a sort of royal changeling in the lost man or woman in the rain. Do you see that as a peculiarly modern predicament?

STAFFORD: I think you may be getting at something I haven't really shared in my consciousness. Let me take a run at this and ask you to bring me round if I don't see the right nuance here. I don't feel this is especially modern, but I think maybe the perception that it is present might be modern. That is, at the end of that poem, the person has to say—and this is a story that could be true and I mean it to be true for anyone—that they can't say this isn't true; they have to say, "Maybe I'm a king." That, because of what we know or how we feel about the nature of things now, it's harder for us to separate out with our fallible ways of judging those who, as a matter of fact, are real royalty, as seen by God. Royalty is an image here, those who have value. Who knows who has value?

In a way it's the same kind of fallibility that I am positing in something like "Staring at Souvenirs of the West." Maybe we're worshipping the wrong people or the wrong things. I have a poem that says something at the end about a real war, how hard it is to find out who the enemy really is. And human beings are all too much given to falling into situations in which they shrug off the need to keep on judging where the danger is, and they go gung-ho for something they quickly agree on as the enemy and have a great big whooping match out of pursuing them, and not till later do they find out, that wasn't it. So, something like "A Story That Could Be True" is especially poignant now, I think, not because it couldn't have been true other times. It could have been, but now we know more it could be true.

And I assume that if one holds himself or herself in that posture, there might be a greater readiness to value the perception of royalty of the right sort rather than having to trust some prescribed system of what is right and wrong?

STAFFORD: Yes, we are always in the process of locating real royalty, not just an election now and then, not just a prize that settles it for us. We are always making that winnowing out. And this afternoon when I was talking to the students in composition, I felt baffled. I don't think I got going at all, but I felt, glimmering beside me, the possibility of locating something for all these people who are subjected to a system that identifies quality in someone as identified by a teacher. Identified by somebody else. Identified by a culture. I wanted those individuals to see the possibility that anyone who says anything to them, or anyone who writes anything may have a contribution that they could see. So when I said I'd read a person's paper, I'd not say, "I can't understand this." It's my business to understand it. It has a meaning. It has a value to me because it's different. And it may be *the* difference.

So once you adopt this assumption about being a king, you have to award it to everyone?

STAFFORD: Yes, to everybody. Yes. It's a story that could be true for anyone. And I think it's partly—I could almost say it here, what I haven't said before, I guess—at least I feel the ambition to accomplish it. If you realize how fallible we are, you realize that a crucial revision in our opinions is always possible. So you're always alert. (A chuckle)

You use the word "dream" frequently. In an interview you are asked to recall the experience that led to the poem "Accountability," and you "dream" your way back to Gillette, Wyoming. In "Vocation" you speak of, "The dream the world is having about itself." You say in "An Introduction to Some Poems" that we must "dream the exact dream to round out" our lives, then "live that dream into stories. . . ." Would you speak about dreaming a little?

STAFFORD: Yes, I've heard, though a long time after I'd already overused this word, that back in Chaucer's day they had a number of words for dreaming, that to be accurate about what you bring to consciousness from dreams, you really need several words. There are different kinds of dreams. Now, I suppose we could say "deep dream" or "work dream," something near to what we've been doing during the day. I mean we could dream when we are asleep something related to bafflements of the day before, closely and obviously related to what we've been doing. Or we could have even daydreams, but there are various ways to dream, or degrees of consciousness about dreams.

When I use those words like "dream my way back to Gillette," I guess I was looking for a term that would signify, all right, I'm going back, I'm recollecting, but I'm not recollecting just with my sharp conscious self to bring into full glare my rational existence, but I'm trying to approximate the feelings I had. Maybe I'm even trying to pick up something from that experience that I didn't get at the time. It's more than just recollection. It's like trying to live it again, so as to have more of it than my fallible self at the time brought to consciousness. I was looking for some term like that. I don't know what term to use, so I said I'll "dream my way back." It's not less than recollection, but more than recollection.

So the uses of "dream" are not necessarily a single feeling or notion?

STAFFORD: No, that's right. It's a whole area of possible realizations that I don't have a better word for. So I'm never accurate, nor do I pretend to be accurate, with words. It occurs to stop here and quote somebody. I remember reading some philosopher named John Wisdom who said, "If we are always sure of the exact meanings of our words and they are unchanging and clear, then how can we use those words when we meet a situation that is new? (Laughter)

I found myself asking this question in another context earlier today. In a poem called "At the Klamath Berry Festival," you envy an Indian dancer, "the places he had not been." I wondered what "places" you had in mind?

STAFFORD: Well, I guess I envied him his condition of not being educated to give quick responses to complicated events in terms of standard workaday solutions. To stay richly baffled is better than to toss off some term for a situation and think you've solved it. Or have some kind of lingo way . . . or some, some automatic adjustment to accommodate to the rich confusion of events sometimes.

I have a story that might help on this. I was walking onto the campus at the University of Alaska early one June morning. That means the sun's rays are a long slant. The light is just sort of coming on, a rheostat up there. And I was looking for a certain building, the Gruening Building—he was a governor of Alaska and there's a building named for him. I was looking for this word, so I'd know where I was. And I suddenly realized, if I didn't know how to read, I'd be seeing this campus. You know, I'd been to school, so I couldn't see the University of Alaska. All I could see was words. And I felt bereft, so I stopped and didn't look for the word. You know, tried to let the scene of that early morning come. It was that sort of thing for the war chief. He still had the whole thing because he didn't have the short circuits.

I wonder if this is part of that revolutionary message you were speaking of earlier. In what sense do you hold the belief in a poem called "A Message from the Wanderer" that one day, "all we have said and all we have hoped/ will be all right"? The poem ends:

Now—these few more words, and then I'm
gone: Tell everyone just to remember
their names, and remind others, later, when we
find each other. Tell the little ones
to cry and then go to sleep, curled up
where they can. And if any of us get lost,
if any of us cannot come all the way—
remember: there will come a time when
all we have said and all we have hoped
will be all right.

There will be that form in the grass.
(*Stories That Could Be True* 10)

STAFFORD: Yes. Other people have charged me in that poem with having just taken an easy way out, saying something optimistic and nice that I couldn't possibly know, or that people couldn't possibly know. Well, I have a wistfulness about that. If charged with that, I can't help agreeing. Someone could have a point. I mean that's . . . I don't really have any insight about whether it will be all right. But in a sense the living of one's developing life in such a way as not to be afraid, as not to assume that it will be bad, is just as possible as assuming it will be bad. So one of my little ways to get along is to say that I don't know enough to be a pessimist. You know, I'm not that sure it's going to be bad. So it would be quite possible to seem tough-minded and say it's going to be bleak, but it's no more accurate than saying it's going to be all right. I don't think either way is within the power of a human being to know. Or maybe . . . in one of my poems today I said, "Maybe those who sang were the lucky ones." I think that's as convincing a "maybe" as the other way.

It's curious to me in that poem that you associate this kind of assertion with the process of perception about what is not obvious about the world—suddenly this antelope appears:

You can pass an antelope and not know
and look back, and then—even before you see—
there is something wrong about the grass.
And then you see. (*Stories That Could Be True* 10)

There's an interesting link there because at the end of this, after you say it may be all right, you say, "There will be that form in the grass."

STAFFORD: Oh, yes. If you look at the grass a certain way, you see it, see the commitment to them helps us to realize what's there. So it's a positive poem at the end, "Message From the Wanderer."

By the way, this is sort of ... just a side remark. But I was down in El Paso starting the reading, and I knew I was going to end with that, "Message From the Wanderer," and a couple had a baby there. The baby began to cry and they didn't want to interrupt the reading, and I stopped and I said, "It's all right to take the baby out, but be sure to have it back for the last because we need it." Because in that poem it says, "Tell the little ones to curl up/ where they can," and so on. (Laughter) I just wanted to have something that would embrace everybody.

Yes. In your work there is this wonderful sort of larger principle of trusting in your own feelings, the things you've said today about writing, that teachers should not do things to instill an individual's distrust of self. The way that respect for persons confirms and supports the "Story That Could Be True" possibility, that "maybe I'm a king." Royalty could be anywhere. I think of something you said once about walking with your father and his saying to you something like, "Bill, keep your eyes open because you might see the hawk first." You latched on to that possibility that, yes, you might.

STAFFORD: That sounds helpful and valid. I was trying to find my way to a formulation this afternoon that would convince those students.

Well, I think you did it clearly. I keep seeing these connections in what you say. I wonder about one other element in these poems we've been talking about. Do you equate a certain kind of freedom with the ability to camouflage yourself—the antelope, the lizard? (Stafford chuckles)

STAFFORD: You make me think about other things that came up earlier today. The idea of protecting yourself by inventions, of being unidentifiable because you are many. I'm thinking about that formulation I had for a student that I was telling you about. Some people say, "How can you be a poet? That's so revealing." And I say, "How can you not be a poet because you haven't invented any masks?" You know, just the opposite of what they are saying. My assumption is that an alive person has many thoughts, is many people, has many attitudes, not one. The arrival at an authentic, true self isn't my idea of what a human being can do. You're going to be different under every circumstance. So this gives me all sorts of trouble with people like Orwell and others who feel that there is such a thing as being honest and dishonest. I can't quite see that. It seems to me, for instance, that the term "euphemism" is a very helpful thing. It's one step toward

96

civilization. (Laughter) If you don't feel you need to use euphemism, then you're a real brute. But to lie a little bit is a sign of your need for redemption. Something like that. I think this is related somehow, that human beings don't find inflexible, everlasting stances. Any individual is different at different times. It sort of goes back to the John Wayne, Buffalo Bill thing too. My heroes are Sancho Panza-like people, really. Don Quixote-like people.

Okay. A reviewer of A *Glass Face in the Rain* went to some lengths to cast you as a sort of Robert Frost of the plains. How do you respond to that sort of comparison?
STAFFORD: Well, I think when you write or when you discourse, write or talk, you need temporary formulations to use on the way to fuller understandings. So a formulation like this doesn't have to be true to be helpful. It's one of the things to say—I think it's an interesting thing to say, myself—and I can see why a person says it, without my feeling that I have to go on to say that's exactly right or that's true except in this and this and this. I'd have to go on for a long time to make the modifications. But you can't say everything at once, so that's something for a reviewer to say. I feel calm about it. I don't think Frost would (a chuckle), but I do.

I've always sensed a sort of predisposition for pessimism in Frost that I would not associate with your work.

STAFFORD: Yeah, I sense that in Frost much more so than in myself. If I get reckless now, and I might as well, it might be revealing, no matter how grotesque it is. I think Frost is much more pessimistic than I am. I think that he is much softer than I, though. He still seemed to believe in fixed things. But I don't.

Would you say that he is, in some ways, more vulnerable?

STAFFORD: Yes. Sentimental. Vulnerable. He's not, uh . . . he's not yielding enough to survive in the world as it is. Oh, I once heard someone, I think it was Gerald Heard, say, "Only saints are hard all the way through" (A chuckle) Well, Frost is no saint, and he's crusty, but the pie's pretty soft inside. Of course, Frost may be a strange one to say that about, but Hemingway was a spectacular example of a crusty meringue pie.

You came close to this earlier today, too. I have students who want to re-write "Traveling Through the Dark" and have the man take some action to save the unborn fawn. What would you say to them?

STAFFORD: One thing I would say is that the assumption that something can be done in extreme circumstances like that is the assumption that neglects the difference between real time and effective time. That is …. Well, you know the idea of the "specious present"? This is the idea that something is going on to the point at which nothing is going to change it, and you feel: It hasn't happened yet; therefore, there's something that can be done, but in effect it's already happened. And the example I heard someone say is, you're standing on board the *Queen Mary*. It's going full speed. About fifty yards from the dock the captain turns to you and says, "You take over." (Laughter) According to some people's way of thinking, okay, there's time to do something. But the captain knows and you know and God knows there's no time. It's all over. So it was all over for the deer.

So if I were talking to students and we had a lot of time, we could talk about the specious present. And there are people who kid themselves all their lives about this, and there are some others who know that there are openings and closures of opportunity that are like a steel trap. You can kid yourself if you want to, but if you don't want to, how about doing something else?

I wonder if their desire blocks out other possibilities. If their desire to act in the specious present isn't a kind of John Wayne reaction?

STAFFORD: I think it is, yeah. In fact, I've had trouble with people in political discussions about pacificism. I remember once taking a stand: Well, I can't stop war. Jesus couldn't stop war. Eisenhower couldn't stop war. Why should I blame myself for not stopping war? What I can do is, to do the things that are within my power. I can decide there's one person who won't be in it. That's a possibility. But I can't stop it, and someone who was there kept saying, "Well, that answer's not good enough for me." You know, he had this John Wayne reaction: "I'm going to stop it." That leads you to terrorist acts that don't really do any good, but they relieve your conscience. I don't want to relieve my conscience; I want to do good.

What would you say to the young man or woman in the wilds of Kansas who yearns to write and is reading this interview?

STAFFORD: I would say that, by all means, if you have tasted the pleasure, the exhilaration, the richness of writing or doing other arts, that's great, that you should. Don't pay any attention to those people who say, "You're unrealistic to do this. You're doomed, unless you get somewhere else," and so on. Write where you are. Write how you are. These things can combine to give you immediate satisfaction that will lead, maybe, to the kinds of satisfactions that are also accompanied by publication, and a lot of it, maybe. But you shouldn't guide yourself by the calculation toward that. Art is something that is satisfying while you are doing it. And to try to put its satisfaction outside itself in terms of recognition a long time later is to change it into something that isn't art.

I think I would add one other thing. It's just really another way of getting at what I'm saying here, and that is: Whatever you do turn out is of possible interest to the kind of people who interest you. Don't assume that what you write, for instance, should go to magazines or editors you can't find any other connection with, except that they have a lot of money or run a big magazine. That's not the way to do it. You get published the way you make friends. You interchange with people who are on your wavelength.

THE ROAD TO CONVICTION:
WILLIAM STAFFORD

By Steven Hind

"Been on probation most of my life. And
the rest of my life been condemned. So these moments
count for a lot—peace, you know." ("Just Thinking" 32)

Imagine you have been working in the hills of California at a
Conscientious Objector camp. It is 1942, January, and you are
looking forward to a week's furlough with a group of pacifist
friends, laying aside your labors and going to Trabuco College to
see a thinker and writer named Gerald Heard.

On the last day of work before your departure, you experience
something so fine that in hindsight it stands as an emblem for the
week to come:

> We worked in snow that day. First the far peaks grew vague;
> then the intervening sweep of space received a tremendous
> gentleness—spaced, slow flakes, thicker and thicker. We saw
> the evergreens whiten gradually, aloof in the lazy fall; and
> when we looked straight up, the flakes were falling dark from
> nowhere, down, down, into our eyes. Our trail along the
> mountain became a long aisle through a remoteness, and we
> walked back to the truck without talking. It was as if
> something were trying to make up to the world for a great loss,
> and to put it to sleep. (*Down in My Heart* 38)

Then Bill Stafford and his fellows drive to a grove of live oaks, get
out of their two cars, and hike up a winding road to a hilltop and
the college. Here they find a collection of buildings: a subsistence
ranch-college presided over by a man with "a sandy emphatic
goatee, a corn-silky mustache, and a quizzical intent expression"
who ladles out soup to the company (39). For a week Stafford
inhabits a small private room here. In meditations (Stafford says
his were "uneventful") and group discussion led by Heard, the
group explores spiritual terrain, and it is clear that this will prove a
confirming, if not formative, experience for Stafford. He

compensates for "the blanks I drew in meditation by jotting down, in a scrawl by firelight, the trend of Gerald Heard's remarks." He includes, "'Understanding is the sympathy of the mind. ...'" and "'The only people who can get things done are those who don't aim directly at getting those things done. The only way to pursue happiness is to pursue something else, and it comes over the shoulder....'" and "'The only person hard all the way through is a saint. The Roman Empire fell ... by a failure of nerve.'" And Stafford adds, "Many of his phrases we found useful later, and they give an indication of the flow and direction of the talks: illumined spirit, inwardly profitable, the way of wonder, alert passivity, anonymous memories, the love offensive, divine incarnation" (44-5).

Stafford adds of Gerald Heard, "As he talked along he would sometimes bring our attention sharply to a height of anticipation: 'Suddenly everything is lit with a terrifying heightening of significance'" (45).

Heard discusses the concept of the "'specious present'"—that the individual cannot be expected, nor expect of himself, to enter into the moment's irresistible momentum and redirect an inevitable disaster not of his own making. Heard's "other contribution," Stafford says, "was a little more disconcerting." How to defend oneself against the charge of "cowardly or dumb" behavior as a Conscientious Objector? Stafford recounts Heard's advice: "'Yes, it is true' (as great men have said before) 'I am a frail vessel in which to transport the truth; but I cannot unsee what I see. ...'"

In the chapter "We Built a Bridge" of Stafford's autobiography *Down In My Heart* appear the basic tenants of his stance through a great many poems, among them some of the best known poems of our time. His truths are there, waiting, for those who "wake up before other people" ("Freedom" 142).

On a February day forty-two years later, William Stafford sat in my living room in Hutchinson, Kansas, responding to my questions about his poetry, especially "Traveling Through the Dark" (77). He said,

> You know the idea of the "specious present"? This is the idea
> that something is going on to the point at which nothing is
> going to change it, and you feel, it hasn't happened yet;
> therefore, there's something that can be done, but in effect it's

already happened. … And there are people who kid themselves all their lives about this, and there are some others who know that there are openings and closures of opportunity that are like a steel trap. You can kid yourself if you want to, but if you don't want to, how about doing something else?

So there it was, the reiteration of what a young man from Kansas, dislocated by war but unshakable in his convictions, had heard confirmed so many years ago on the West Coast, far from his home. Stafford gathered his convictions from his own family spirit in Kansas, no doubt, but he confirmed his compass heading in California. And he steered true to his course right through to the end, "Getting used to being a person/ taking it easy, you know" ("Emily, This Place, and You" 35).

10 October 1997

Stafford, William. *Down in My Heart: Peace Witness in War Time*. 1947. Rpt. Corvallis: Oregon State University, 2006.

---. *The Way It Is: New & Collected Poems*. St. Paul: Graywolf Press, 1998.

VI. WRITERS ON WILLIAM STAFFORD

TALK TO STRANGERS AND STOP ON BY

By Robert Day

At the Library of Congress in 1994 there was a tribute to William Stafford, the American poet who, in 1970, had been what is now called the poet laureate of the United States. There were the usual accolades: Bill Stafford was a poet whose plain language fitted his flatland Kansas sensibility. His poems were gifts to all Americans, not just to other poets or professors of literature.

There were other kind words: About the self-evident and the oblique stories in his poems. About those poems' gifted reticence. Then something extraordinary was said. One of his children, his daughter Kit, I think, told us of her father's repeated advice to them as they were growing up: "Talk to strangers."

Not far from where I live when in Kansas, and about the same distance from where Bill Stafford grew up, there is a high school in a town of about a thousand that has a video security system of which they are especially proud. I had been asked to be part of a literary program there, and I noticed the surveillance camera in the room we used. Later I saw the black-and-white glow of monitors in the school's office. I watched pictures of the gymnasium (empty this autumn Saturday), various hallways (also empty), our meeting room (adults milling around drinking coffee), and finally an outside shot: the wide prairie as background, a small Kansas town in the foreground.

One of the school's officials and a parent stopped to say that you couldn't be too careful these days, what with Columbine and Amber Alert. Bad things happen in schools. And out of schools. Better to be vigilant than sorry. When they left, I could see them on the monitors as they walked across the lawn. They talked for a moment over the bed of a pickup truck and then drove off — safe, I suppose, in the knowledge that someone might have been watching them.

I was Bill Stafford's student because I learned from him about writing and life: Do it all and do it all now. The beginning may not be the beginning. The end may not be the end. These aphorisms applied not only to his craft and mine, but to the way we lived.

Over the years we wrote back and forth: letters, postcards, copies of our work. As he was one of the most prolific American poets of the 20th century, I got plenty more of the latter than he did. No matter how far apart we were, Bill in Oregon and me in Kansas or in Europe, he would sign off with "Adios" or "Cheers." Then, as if we were just across the pasture, he'd add: "Stop on by." My feeling now is that when I'd get to him, a little windblown and dusty from the walk over, he'd want to know if I'd met any strangers on the way, and what stories they had to tell.

What kind of America have we become when it seems stupid to give the same advice to our children that Bill Stafford gave his? Talk to strangers? Have we come to believe that surveillance cameras in the high schools of tiny towns are necessary to teach our students the eternal vigilance they'll need to live in towns beyond their own? Or in their own? What with Columbine and Amber Alert. Or would we be better off to listen to Bill Stafford from his poem "Holcomb, Kansas"?

> Now the wide country has gone sober again.
> The river talks all through the night, proving
> its gravel. The valley climbs back into its hammock
> below the mountains and becomes again only what
> it is: night lights on farms make little blue domes
> above them, bring pools for the stars; again
> people can visit each other, talk easily,
> deal with real killers only when they come.

Unless, of course, we have all become real killers.

There may be no reclaiming Bill Stafford's vision of America, but don't you remember that once upon a time, in his plain voice, he spoke for you?

CONTEMPORARY PROFILES: WILLIAM STAFFORD (April 1993)

By Linda Rodriguez

Looking back over a distinguished career as a major American poet, William Stafford cannot pinpoint a beginning time for his writing. "Everyone writes when they're little kids in school," he notes. "I didn't start writing; the others just stopped for some reason. I loved it too much to stop."

Growing up in Kansas, Stafford wanted to be an explorer. "But once I had to think about earning a living, I thought that writing would be a fun way to do it," he says. "I took courses in writing specialized articles in college. I could see myself taking a notebook and traveling all over, and it sounded great."

Stafford points out that his desire to explore and travel did not stem from dislike of his native state. He lived all over Kansas as he grew up and sees himself as having been completely under the influence of Kansas until after he was in graduate school. "I had to be drafted to finally leave," he says.

Although it may seem a leap for the kid who wanted to travel the world writing articles for a living to have gained his reputation as a poet, Stafford points out that he has written more nonfiction than most readers realize. His first book, *Down In My Heart* (The Bench Press), was nonfiction, written about his experiences as a conscientious objector in World War II. "It's still in print," he says. "Every time there's a war, they reissue it. I wish it would go out of print, become obsolete."

Besides his books and articles on writing, Stafford has also written a book on teaching, his second vocation, *Friends to This Ground* (National Council for Teachers s English). He came to teaching after working a variety of jobs to support his wife and four children. "Oh, I worked oil refinery and Forest Service jobs, worked in the sugar beet fields, too," he remembers. "Then I tried teaching and found that I liked to teach, and I might even get good at it someday. I think I finally did get to be pretty good, learned effective ways to present things and all, right before I retired."

Writing poetry came directly from Stafford's struggle to support his family. "Long before I began teaching, I began to write poetry," he says. "I would get up in the morning before going to whatever job I was working, and I would write. The poetry came from getting up in the morning and writing in my journal. I developed short pieces from that early-morning journal work, and sometimes I could convince some editor that they were poems, and he would publish them."

Stafford's early poetry met with success, and he published individual poems in many journals, but he was in his forties before he published his first book of poetry. "I just collect them until I have enough for a manuscript," he says. "Sooner or later, they add up."

Stafford read the journals of Emerson and other writers early in his life, and now the thought of his own unpublished journals from years of early mornings on the living-room couch with paper and a clipboard must intrigue writers of a later generation who share his interest in reading about how a writer goes about doing his work. He prefers to write in the morning because early morning is when new things come to him. His habit since 1942 has been to write every day.

"You don't have to be heroic," Stafford says. "Just be persistent. Stay with it. I've found you lose it otherwise. You tell yourself you'll remember whatever it is until you start writing again, but you don't. I lost good ideas that way until I started writing every morning."

Such regular habits have enabled Stafford to keep several books going at once most of the time. His latest, *Who Are You Really, Wanderer?* (forthcoming from Honeybrook Press), was written at the same time he was completing the manuscript, *Sometimes I Breathe*, which he will submit to Harper's when enough time has passed since his last book came out from that publisher.

"I've had a steady relationship with Harper's since the 1960s and have no desire to jump ship or anything," he says. "It's worked well for them and me, and that's what counts."

Stafford takes the same attitude when asked about the value of academic creative writing programs. He has had good experiences with them, although he recognizes that they may have drawbacks. "But so do regular academic programs," he adds. "The competition can get real bad in both writing and academic programs, but that doesn't negate the benefits they can offer.

Being in a writing program can offer that little extra incentive to turn out work that can be crucial for a lot of people. I was already writing regularly when I got there, but other people really needed that incentive."

Stafford has over thirty books of poems, and his numerous honors include the National Book Award and 1991 NEA Senior Fellowship. A recent collection, *My Name Is William Tell* (Confluence Press), was published in 1992.

Stafford's lifelong involvement in the peace movement— though more than fifty years of membership in The Fellowship of Reconciliation, shared with his wife, and in his major involvement in founding American Writers Against the Vietnam War— emerges as a major theme in his work. He has even published a book, *A Scripture of Leaves,* with the publishing house of the Church of the Brethren, one of the three "peace churches" in America.

"I guess there is a kind of peace and violence concern that's a recurrent flavor in my writing," he says. "It's hard for me to say, though. It always feels like something new. I try for some kind of balance, playfulness, irony, some way to make a poem an experience for a reader. I don't believe it's my place to force feed information to people or preach or anything. I care, and that shows through. I guess I'd like to have a serenity or acceptance about me. I wish I did have that, and wisdom. Know the things you can do something about, and what you can't and accept it."

Stafford's advice to beginning writers echoes this striving for the ability to accept life. "It's stuff you hear everywhere," he says. "Keep a journal. Lower your standards so you can keep going. Don't get competitive. That's a real trap. Don't pay attention to editors' and publishers' rejections. Know where you want to go and keep going. Maybe after awhile, the publishers will catch up with you."

KIM STAFFORD INTERVIEW

By Kirsten Bosnak

Poet and essayist Kim Stafford came to the Flying W Ranch near Cottonwood Falls, Kansas, for the 2008 William Stafford Rendezvous, a celebration of his father's work and influence. We talked on Saturday morning, April 12, in the gathering room of the ranch guesthouse. We got started about eight o'clock as the sun shone through the big east windows.

At the beginning of *Early Morning*, you describe a dream you had on the morning of the day your father died. It was a dream of a father lost, and you wrote it down in your notebook. What are your thoughts are about the importance of paying attention to our dreams?

KIM STAFFORD: To me, dreams are the sustaining reminder that human beings are created to understand life by story — by image, by often-strange, resonant detail. When I teach writing, people say, "Well, I can't think of anything to write" or "My life doesn't make sense." And I feel like the dreaming mind is a kind of internal teacher, oracle, shaman, minister even — putting forth constantly, abundantly, poetic experience. So you wake up from a dream and ... Part of the early morning experience for me is to stay close to that intuitive experience of dreaming. When you first wake, there is kind of unexplained clarity—and before we get too caught up in the business of the world or turn on the radio or get out that to-do list, that calendar, that schedule —to remain in that realm of immanence, where one simple thing may be of great importance. . . .

Did you talk to your father about how he would approach dreams and his sharing of dreams?

KIM STAFFORD: I didn't talk to him about it, but in his daily writings, quite often he would write down a dream as a way to get going. You imagine, he's there, in his case, three or four in the morning, and it's utterly quiet, he won't be disturbed for several hours, and so, how do you get started? Well, one way is, before you start thinking, do some remembering. And maybe the most immediate memory is a dream. So he would jot down, in a few sentences, some enigmatic dream. Many of his dreams were about teaching. He dreamed the standard teacher's anxiety dream: I can't find the classroom; I'm not ready; I read the wrong text; who are these strange people that I'm supposed to teach? Long after he retired, he kept dreaming that. But he would write it down. He wouldn't use it in his writing often, but sometimes there will be one little detail in a dream that will show up in his poem.

Your father writes in *The Answers Are Inside the Mountains*, "In everyone's life, there's all this torrent of things happening and a writer ... would be someone who pays attention, and close attention at least at intervals, to that torrent. Or a writer is not someone who has to dream of things to write, but has to figure out what to pick up out of the current as it goes by." I wondered how you decide what to pick up out of the current, how you decide something is worth writing about.

KIM STAFFORD: Well, this is maybe an odd example, but we got to the Flying W yesterday, and we stepped out of the car, and I looked down, and there was an arrow point on the ground. It was about the size of my little fingernail. It was blood red. And we all stood there amazed. Now, that's unusual, but my feeling is, if the arrowhead hadn't been there to distract me, I might have seen something more ordinary but more important. My father used to say, if the first line you think of to write is a good line, it's probably not yours. [Laughing] And he didn't trust good lines; he wanted to start with something very simple.

So, for me, if I look out from the bunkhouse here, it's maybe the slouch of the gate at the corral — that beautifully undulating, sagging line of the old pine pole that they hung up there a long time ago — that catches my eye. Or in conversation, people are talking along, and something catches your ear — the way my Aunt Mar in Nickerson has a whole repertoire of ways to say the word: yy-yeh-ess, yy-yes! And that catches my ear, so out of the torrent of conversation, the visible, things you touch and so on, it seems that there are certain friendly particulars that ... Would it be too strong to say, they are yearning to be noticed? That's what I feel.

And I think we're back to Nietzsche, my father's feeling that for Nietzsche the torrent of life is filled with little handshakes of ideas that are reaching out toward you.

And my own formulation for this is that a writer doesn't have to be smart, but only alert. You don't have to be in possession of brilliant ideas; you only have to be aware of the amazing things that are.

This is a question about something I remember particularly from the first time I read *Early Morning*. In the chapter "Sleeping On Hillsides," you say that your parents "entrusted [you] to the dark," that they let you sleep out alone as a child; they wouldn't question you when you came in at odd hours from some pretty extraordinary night-time exploration; and even would let you start out early, during cross-country trips with the family, ahead of the car, on foot along the highway in the predawn darkness. How did that kind of free exploration, with their blessing, influence your life as an artist?

KIM STAFFORD: That amazes me. I mean, we'd be crossing the continent, and we'd stop in a little town way out in the open country, and it was okay for me to get up in the dark and start walking in the direction of our journey.

How old are we talking about?

KIM STAFFORD: Well, probably twelve, fourteen. Just set out along the road, with the sense, that, well we know which road we're gonna be on, and so, as far as you get, that's where we'll find you. I couldn't do that with my own son. I feel bad about that. Has the world changed? Am I more timid than my parents? It goes with my parents, both of them, saying, when we would be out in the world, "Don't forget to talk to strangers" — sort of the opposite of frequent advice. Because if you don't talk to strangers, how can you find your way, how can you learn anything?

We never talked about it this way, but there is a danger — you might get lost, you might meet the wrong person — but if you don't go forth freely, you might not meet the world. You might not become who you are to become. And I think that quiet but persistent danger is part of the bargain my parents were ready

115

strike with the world.

It's highly symbolic — them allowing you to go out like that.

Well, you know, I think we're back to freedom. Freedom can be an unused gift lying on the ground beside you. "I could be free, I could do this if I wanted, if I got up early enough, if I put in the effort, if I were brave enough to challenge the ideas of others," and so on. But freedom isn't real unless it's practiced. And that can be the physical freedom of going forth into the dark, or that can be freedom of ideas, of exploring things — like my father's phrase, "the unknown good in our enemies" — with your mind, of going into the dark, of going past the easy signposts of unexamined patriotism or sort of supposed national interests....

Everybody who's coming to the Flying W today has been inspired by your father's poetry, but nobody has explored his life and writing as deeply as you have. Since his death, what do you continue to learn from his life and his writing?

KIM STAFFORD: Well, first I'd like to say that we don't know if no one has explored as deeply! I've explored as deeply as I can, Kim, the son, the literary companion in many ways. I did have a chance to go out with my father on the road to all kinds of programs and so on, but that doesn't mean that someone, maybe who never met him, encountered in his poetry dimensions of experience that I will never know. I think one of the amazing, miraculous, lucky things about reading is: You can encounter another person in a way that may not have been possible in person. I imagine someone in a difficult time of their life searching for answers, searching for direction, coming upon a poem by William Stafford or someone else and finding there the beginning of a remedy. I think people's lives can be saved by encountering the right poem at the right time.

"Some time when the river is ice/ask me mistakes I have made. Ask me whether/ what I have done is my life." You know that William Stafford poem, "Ask Me?" I can imagine someone coming upon that poem and suddenly being liberated from a kind of false accountability and given back an opportunity to live their own life in their own way. That could save your life, not in the sense that you were going to physically die, but, spiritually, people die all the time, and a poem can bring that back.

How do you account for his kind of spiritual courage?

KIM STAFFORD: Oh — there is no accounting for it. There's this story that I tell in *Early Morning*. He goes off to school as very young child in Hutchinson. And he comes home and tells his mother that there were these new kids in school, who were black, who were up against a wall being taunted by the others. And his mother says, "What did you do, Billy?" "Well, I went and stood by them."

Well, how do you account for that? Where did he get the notion that one should do that, *could* do that, that he personally could do that, no matter what happened? His first word was "moon" — now, how do we account for that? What does that mean? He had parents who were poor and not broadly educated, but curious, attentive, loved to talk recklessly, fought over books from the library — who gets to read that one first? — eager for discovery. So he had the early cradle of a good situation and a lively family, but as to why he came forth ... I have one little clue about him. I went out to Liberal High School, where he graduated in 1932, and I met with his classmates, and one, a wonderful old lady... I said, "Do you remember William Stafford?" And she said, "Oh yes, he always kept to himself, he was different" — you know, these code words we use for the loner. "But," she said, "Miss Arington saw that he had something unusual." Now, Miss Arington was a legend in that school who taught for thirty years or so. And, you know, one teacher can make a big difference.

I'm clutching at tentative hints here, so we can't answer that question except maybe by going into the poetry, his accounts: "Our mother knew our worth — not much"; the world was "a world of our betters" ... That sense of a kind of brutal modesty. And his poem, "Serving with Gideon": and after all, "I was *almost* one. ... I was *almost* one of the boys." You know, that sense of being outside, which is a tough gig when you're young, but for a poet, it can be an enriching predicament to be at the edge of things, to not be given abundance easily and needing to find your own.

Is it tough — I mean, do you get tired of talking about your father?

KIM STAFFORD: Not at all! I love my daddy. I'll tell you kind of a spooky thing that happened to me a few years ago. I was talking to an old friend, a man who had been my teacher in college, poetry teacher, Ralph Salisbury, and he said, "Kim, there's something I've thought about telling you for some years now, and I didn't know if I should."

[Laughing] And I leaned forward and said, "Well, Ralph, times a'wasting!" and he said, "You know, years ago, your father and I were on a long drive. We were going to a program somewhere at night, and we got to talking about our children, and your father said, 'Well, I love all my children, but there is one who is myself, and that's Kim.'"

I said, "Oh, Ralph, I can see why you kept that under your hat for a while." I don't know if that's something I didn't already know, in a way. You know, my dad and I were very different, but we had a kind of reckless abandon and a kind of trust in going anywhere — out wandering through the world, and in language, too. That's a mystery.

I think people know that, and I think that's why they keep asking you to come.

KIM STAFFORD: I'll go anywhere. My mother says, maybe it's time for you to let go of Bill. And my feeling is, well, why would I do that? Nietzsche said, "Some people are born posthumously." There's an example of a Nietzschean wild thing to say. And I feel that — I wouldn't say this directly to my mother — but my response is, Have you noticed there's a war on? Have you noticed that my father's peaceful words are an elixir in times like these, that not only individual souls, but whole nations are lost? And if traveling with my father's notions of reconciliation and listening and opening your life to the stranger and seeking the unknown good in your enemy can be part of our fate as humans, what other work would I do?

The book of your father's early poems, *Another World Instead*, has just come out, and it's great timing. What would you like

118

to say about this new collection, and what are some of the current projects at the William Stafford Archive?

KIM STAFFORD: I think the new collection sort of circles back to where we started, because the full line that that title comes from is, "I dream another world instead." These are poems William Stafford wrote between 1937 and 1947. He's just starting out. It includes the poem that he identifies as: This is the first time I tried to express myself in poetry, written in study hall at KU, 1937. So here's this young person coming out of the Depression, drifting toward war, as everyone knew, and in that dark, difficult time, he is starting to practice his writing.

Some of the poems are clunkers, I would have to say, but they're all interesting as evidence of someone finding a practice that will lead to amazing things. I think I take up that book the way he took up the practice of writing: Do you stop because every episode in your learning is not demonstrably successful? No. You welcome every stage. There are many interesting poems. You see his devotion to hometown, to friendship, to ideas, to peacemaking, sense of place. You see him kind of staking out his territory as a writer and as a human being.

My own dream for the archive is to create something that doesn't exist except in my mind at this point: what I call the William Stafford Studio for Reconciliation. This would be an online set of resources where you could find the digitized first draft of any William Stafford poem. And you could then walk through the revisions with him, and then you could hear him read the poem. We have ninety CDs of his readings, all indexed. Do you want to hear the twenty-five times we have recorded of him reading "Traveling Through the Dark" or the twenty times he read "Ask Me"? So you can accompany William Stafford in the creation of one of his poems. And then the next step would be the most important: a set of invitations, prompts, openings for your own writing, for discussion, for being a witness for peace.

My mom calls this the impossible dream, but I think it's the possible dream. I want to make his work available when I'm not here. And I'm not making a big claim that my father is, obviously, the one and only source, but I want to make what's available in his life broadly available to people everywhere. I think that's the work of our time, to put the resources of human conversation forth.

119

BILL STAFFORD AND THE MUTTON CHOP

By Ralph Salisbury

In one of his published letters, Ezra Pound pontificates that one should not write about a great man and a mutton chop without indicating that there is a gulf between the two. Aware of the gulf of death, I pontificate, that it is important to have a role model, a hero, and, for me, as for many others, Bill Stafford is a role model, a hero, someone better than myself, someone to emulate, and, at the same time, he was an unpretentious human being and my friend.

Bill and I first met when he hitched a ride in my '39 Studebaker to Paul Engle's Iowa Writers Workshop party, at Paul's Stone City stone mansion, near Iowa City, on the land where Grant Wood and others had painted and become famous. Bill Stafford was a doctoral candidate, and I was an undergraduate, invited to mingle with the graduates because I'd published in a New York magazine. Bill was not famous, and fame to me was a dream I tried to write into being, wanting—a 20-year-old, mixed-blood, mixed up ex-farmhand, ex-soldier—wanting the Meaning of Life, which literature seemed to promise.

The Writers Workshop party was a bring your own bottle affair, but I was intending to put in an appearance and, then, drive on for a couple of hours to do some weekend work at my parents' farm. "Would you like a drink?" Paul Engle asked, doubtless aware of my awkward egocentricity. When I declined the drink, my hitchhiker protested to Paul, "You didn't offer me a drink." He was right. He'd been standing beside me. He'd been snubbed. Bill published a poem titled – if I remember correctly – "At the Chairman's Housewarming," and the unnamed professor in the poem was not depicted favorably. Years later, Bill told me that Paul said, "Bill, I'm not really like that," and the two of them became friends. Known, justifiably, for his kindness and humility, Bill Stafford was, also, capable of standing up for himself, in poems and in life.

My second meeting with Bill took place in 1961, in Eugene, Oregon, where we were scheduled to make presentations for a

121

teacher's group. It was Armed Forces Day, and, during my presentation, the poems had to compete with a parade. Outside the huge glass window behind my audience's backs, young women appeared. The young women were attired in brief clothing and were twirling batons. Then came the band, complete with many drums. Then the riflemen rang the concrete with their boots. The finale was an elephant parade of tanks, whose cannons approximated the size of telephone poles, their message clear. Throughout my doomed defense of our shared art, Bill Stafford sat grinning, in a glee he shared with our fellow teachers, that his presentation was completed, while his former World War Two volunteer colleague and, since the Korean War, fellow pacifist, had to struggle against the United States Army.

Several times after our first shared event, Bill and I worked together in classrooms, and, of his teaching, I would say what virtually all of his colleagues and former students have said, in their own ways, that he was a concerned, sympathetic and perceptive teacher, who trusted the likelihood that most of his students would have years to go on learning after his final word with them. An alert receptivity to the potential in others informed Bill's teaching, and it also informs his writing. He was not an "easy" teacher and he was not an "easy" poet. He kept to a high literary expectation of himself and others, but he was accessible. He met students and readers in the common ground of language and shared recognitions where each could be his or her best self.

As an editor, I published Bill's work before he was well known, and, after he was famous, he generously gave poems for an anthology of Native American poetry, *A Nation Within*, which I'd been asked to edit for Outriggers Press in New Zealand. Bill had published some poems about Native American concerns and had listed himself as of the "Crowsfeet tribe." When some of my friends objected that there was no "Crowsfeet tribe," I did the obvious thing, I asked Bill, and he said he was only repeating what his father had told him. Young Indians may not realize that, for Indians of my and Bill Stafford's generation, no "cultural advancement" programs were being funded. For those of us who acknowledged our Indian heritage there was, at best, condescension and, often, contempt.

With a little research, I found that Crowfoot was a Seneca leader who had resisted white invaders, and his followers had populated the upstate New York area where Bill Stafford's father had lived, an area in which intermarriage between Indians and whites was not unusual. Crowfoot's resistance group was called Crowfoot's Band, and the distinction between "tribe" and "band" was not the only casualty of the European-American onslaught. It seems logical to assume that Bill Stafford's father was a typical Eastern U.S. mixed-blood, who knew, from family stories, that he was Indian, but, due to the ravages of genocidal conquest, knew little else.

Robert Bly and I talked in Portland, Oregon, after an event to honor Bill Stafford's memory and to celebrate publication of Bill's *Collected Poems,* which Robert had edited. The subject of Bill's Indian blood and poems was mentioned by someone, and Robert revealed that he had written "Crowsfeet Tribe" in the book's introduction, probably following some contributor's note published elsewhere. When I told Robert of my research, he said that, whatever the genealogy, Bill's face was not simply an European American face, and I would add that Bill's vision was a Native American Spirit Vision, as well as an European esthetic vision.

Bill's son Kim has published a book denying Indian blood, so I understand, and, though I have affection for Kim, I suspect that he has confused uncertainty with denial. Bill Stafford's father's assertion is in line with my encyclopedia information, and this seems to be a not unusual case, where ethnic identity lives on in the words of survivors.

Writing as an Indian is only one part of William Stafford's work, but, connecting as it does with the themes of social justice and harmony with nature, it is an important part..

Bill once said to me, "I don't know as I've ever written a poem that could be called great, but I think maybe all of my work, taken together, may amount to something."

I am not Ezra Pound, and the Gulf of Death makes words as insignificant as camera flashes in midday sun, but I would say, "Yes, Bill, your poems evoke Truth, Beauty and Love, and your work amounts to something very good – for all of us – amounts to something great."

WILLIAM STAFFORD: GENIUS IN CAMOUFLAGE

By Jonathan Holden

In 1972, five years before driving to Missoula, Montana, to interview Richard Hugo, I was a student in the Ph.D. program at the University of Colorado. I was driving into Denver with my friend Reg Saner to conduct a Poets-in-the-Schools program. We had turned off U.S. 36 onto I-25 and were heading straight toward downtown Denver when, in one of those moments James Hillman discusses in *The Soul's Code,* dictated, perhaps, by one's daemon, I realized what I should do with my studies — with my life. I should drop the pathetic idea of doing a thesis in medieval literature to please some father figure and instead do a thesis in twentieth-century American literature, about William Stafford. My thesis would be immediately publishable, for there were no books about him. Best of all, I could drive out to Lake Oswego and interview him for the book. I could actually meet him.

The first time I met him was in July 1972 at his house. He was fifty-eight. It was thrilling to meet him, but it was daunting, too, because he was so much like my own father, Alan. Wiry, elfin, with the face of a fox, Stafford was curious about everything around him, absolutely alert. Alan had graduated from Harvard with a B.S. in chemistry in 1925, the year after Stanley Kunitz had. They both graduated summa cum laude. All my life I had been surrounded by Bell Labs physicists gossiping about who was in line for the Nobel Prize this year, who was at Cal Tech, who was at Cambridge at the Cavendish Laboratory, who was at M.I.T. (The gossip of scientists is depressingly similar to the gossip of writers.) Like the Bell Labs scientists, Bill was on the leading edge of his field, lecturing everywhere, everywhere in demand. He was a genius. From being in the presence of Bell Labs geniuses for my entire childhood, I'd learned to recognize them, like a bird-watcher. I had to. It was a kind of survival technique, to avoid making a fool of oneself in the presence of some of the most high-powered intellectuals in the world. Some of them had worked with J. Robert Oppenheimer on the Manhattan Project. Los Alamos had been their vortex.

In his book *Alone with America,* Richard Howard refers to the "arrogant otherness" of the persona in Stafford's first poetry collection, *West of Your City.* It has been pointed out by the poet/critic Judith Kitchen that "West of Your City" alludes to Frost's title *North of Boston.* "Your city" is Boston. "You" is Frost. Howard, the quintessential New Yorker and European traveler, is right, but only partially. Stafford's "otherness" wasn't arrogant. It was the otherness of every major mind I've had the privilege to observe. It was the neutral, appraising, canny posture of intellectuality — an appetite that is aesthetic, amoral, and endlessly curious. And cold. What must have it been like having Stafford as a father? Not easy. It is now legendary how Stafford, so as not to disturb his family, would get up well before dawn to write. He described the routine in his poem "Mornings":

Quiet,
   rested, the brain begins to burn
   and glow like a coal in the dark,
      early—four in the morning, cold, with
   frost on the lawn.

We are familiar, too, with Stafford's cooperative venture with his son Kim: the book *Braided Apart.* We are less familiar with the fact that Stafford's eldest son, Brett, killed himself. Brett must have felt as I did: compared to Alan, I would never measure up. Virtually Alan's last words to me — we were discussing Wittgenstein — were, "Son, until you know German, you'll never understand Western culture."

When Stafford's son Kim visited Kansas State in the fall of 1998, as the primary speaker in a conference in honor of William Stafford, he and I talked about Brett's suicide in 1988. Kim said that the suicide had been about a love affair and that his father had said of Brett: "He wasn't mean enough."

Meanwhile, the mistaken identification of Stafford as a "regional" poet continues: In the *New York Times* obituary of August 31, 1993, the headline read, "William Edgar Stafford, Professor and Poet of the West, Dies at 79." The writer, Wolfgang Saxon, wrote:

Both his life and his writing looked westward or to the Northwest, and he found his themes in small-town family life and in nature. His work was infused with the vast expanses of desert and prairie, mountain ranges and sky.

Like a fox, like a wildcat, Stafford lived his life in camouflage. He camouflaged his true nature. A poem which for me epitomizes this camouflage is his poem "For the Governor" in *Someday, Maybe:*

Heartbeat by heartbeat our governor tours
the state, and before a word and after a word
over the crowd the world speaks to him,
thin as a wire. And he knows inside
each word, too, that anyone says,
another word lurks, and inside that...
Sometimes we fear for him: he, or someone,
must act for us all. Across our space
we watch him while the country leans
on him: he bears time's tall demand,
and beyond our state he must think the shore
and beyond that the waves and the miles and the waves.

On the surface, the poem is about a man campaigning for the governorship of a state like Kansas. But read closely, the poem yields a second meaning. The poem is about the relation of the mind to the body. "Across our space / we watch him while the country leans / on him: he bears time's tall demand." The mind is able to conceive of its end, the body's eventual death. Moreover, the mind is able to conceive of itself: consciousness of consciousness is what makes us particularly human. This, the poem's true issue — Stafford's intellectuality — has been camouflaged. I asked him about a female figure named Ella who appears in some of his poems about rural Kansas life. He remarked that "Ella" is a female third-person pronoun.
A second well-known poem, "Report from a Far Place," camouflages its sophistication in a way that is also typically Staffordean. The poem reads:

Making these word things to
step on across the world, I
could call them snowshoes.
They creak, sag, bend, but
hold, over the great deep cold,
and they turn up at the toes.
In war or city or camp
they could save your life;
you can muse them by the fire.
Be careful though: they
burn, or don't burn, in their own
strange way, when you say them.

At first glance, this poem appears to be about writing, "making word things." Read closely, however, it appears to be more about reading than about writing, especially the lines "In war or city or camp / they could save your life; / you can muse them by the fire." The cleverest line, though, is the offhanded remark "and they turn up at the toes." Often, in Stafford poems, casual asides are profound. If we think of the way in which the turned-up toes of skis or snowshoes deflect the snow, deflect the world, we find a metaphor for the way in which the abstract nature of words deflects the world from us and thus keeps us from suffocating in existence, allowing us to ride "on top of" things momentarily. The title puzzles us, until we remember that in Stafford's symbolic vocabulary "near" means "kindred" and "far" means "different." The "far" place which imposes "word things" upon the world is the mind.

There is another side of Stafford, though, that dispenses with camouflage. It is not affable. It is fierce. We glimpse this side, at the end of "Our City Is Guarded by Automatic Rockets," where he says:

There is a place behind our hill so real
it makes me turn my head, no matter. There
in the last thicket lies the cornered cat
saved by its claws, now ready to spend
all that is left of the wilderness, embracing
its blood. And that is the way I will spit
life, at the end of any trail where I smell any hunter.

The last piece Stafford published before his death was a review of the anthology *Against Forgetting: Twentieth-Century Poetry of Witness,* edited by Carolyn Forché. His approach to the anthology is prickly:

> But there are inherent problems in a collection like this. For instance, the individual glimpses that create the distinction of poetry put a strain on the thesis of the book; books that buckle down to the thesis can hardly attain the shiver of the unexpected that distinguishes lively discourse. We can be informed; we can encounter the thoughts and emotions of significant people...but it takes something more to validate the poetry experience.

And later in the review he writes:

> A further problem above achieving authenticity in a survey like this one lurks everywhere in the selections: quality is primary, but the need for wide representation put a strain on that criterion. And how vividly do you have to suffer in order to qualify? I feel a bump when the explanatory note says, "the Germans decided." All Germans? And similarly when Carolyn Forché says, "My new work seemed controversial to my American contemporaries." (Who, me?) The labels in the book . . . put a torque on me, snagged my attention, kept me wary of living on the emotional high of atrocity hunger.

Morally and intellectually exacting as Stafford's mind was, there was a softer side to him. I glimpsed it most vividly in the summer of 1987 when he and I were on the staff of the Port Townsend Writers Conference. Several of us were being driven back to Fort Worden State Park from dinner at a restaurant. Stafford was in the front seat, Marvin Bell was beside me in the middle seat. As we drove past a brightly lit bar that was the students' hangout, Marvin called to the driver to let him out there. Stafford burst out to Marvin: "Must you?" It was a motherly gesture, pure reflex, like a mother instinctively reaching out to stop a toddler from walking into a busy street. I realized that he loved Marvin.

When, the day after Stafford suffered his heart attack at home,

Henry Taylor called me with the news, my first thought was, "How lucky to go like that, that cleanly," and that Stafford had indeed led a lucky life. He himself had told me as much, years ago at Stephens College, when I had invited him there. I don't remember what I was mumbling to him, but he suddenly faced me and glared at me, pure wildcat: "You don't understand." He hissed it. *"I was just lucky."* He took nothing for granted. And I thought, also, of Willa Cather's famous story "Neighbor Rosicky":

> The old farmer looked up at the doctor with a gleam of amusement in his queer, triangular-shaped eyes.... Rosicky's face had the habit of looking interested — suggested a contented disposition and a reflective quality that was gay rather than grave. This gave him a certain detachment, the easy manner of an onlooker and observer.

The end of the story describes Rosicky's friendship with his daughter-in-law, Polly:

> She had a sudden feeling that nobody in the world, not her mother, not Rudolph, or anyone really loved her as much as old Rosicky did. It perplexed her. She sat frowning and trying to puzzle it out. It was as if Rosicky had a special gift for loving people, something that was like an ear for music or an eye for colour. It was quiet, unobtrusive; it was merely there.... After he dropped off to sleep, she sat holding his warm, broad, flexible brown hand. She had never seen another in the least like it. She wondered if it wasn't a kind of gipsy hand, it was so alive and quick and light in its communications — very strange in a farmer. Nearly all of the farmers she knew had huge lumps of fists, like mauls, or they were knotty and bony and uncomfortable looking, with stiff fingers. But Rosicky's hand was like quicksilver, flexing, muscular,...it was a warm brown   hand, with some cleverness in it,...and something else which Polly could only call "gipsy-like" — something nimble and lively and sure, in the way that animals are.

I would like to imagine that William Stafford died as Rosicky did, as described by Willa Cather:

After he had taken a few stitches, the cramp began in his chest, like yesterday. He put his pipe down cautiously on the window-sill and bent over to ease the pull. No use — he had better try to get to bed if he could. He rose and groped his way across the familiar floor, which was rising and falling like the deck of a ship. At the door he fell. When Mary came in, she found him lying there, and the moment she touched him she knew that he was gone.

In my experience, Cather is the only author to describe accurately, without sentimentality, in the figure of Rosicky, the mysterious, inexplicable quality of human goodness — its elusiveness, its disinterestedness, its absence of vanity. William Stafford understood all this. He lived it. Determined to keep the truth of his genius from embarrassing us, he camouflaged it as carefully, as considerately as he could.

132

AN INTERVIEW WITH ROBERT DAY
ABOUT WILLIAM STAFFORD

By Al Ortolani

The following interview was conducted for The Little Balkans Review *with novelist, short story writer and poet, Robert Day. It took place via email over a period of several days in January and February of 2010. The entire interview is in* LBR *Vol. 6 (2010).*

My first encounter with William Stafford was when I was in high school and I read his poem "Fifteen." As a motorcycle enthusiast and a budding poet, I was charged with the thought that poems could be about something as elemental as a wrecked motorcycle. This opened doors for me into different ways of seeing poetry, and motorcycles even. Can you describe when and where you first met William Stafford? What were your first impressions?

DAY: Professor Edgar Wolfe, my writing teaching at the University of Kansas, brought Bill to campus the fall of 1960. I remember him being a slight and shy man. In those days we thought live poets were Beats and smoked dope. Otherwise, poets were dead and either English or Italian. Before Bill arrived, my friend Harris Flora and I checked out a copy of Bill's poetry and took it over to the Gaslight Tavern where we drank a few Red Beers and read the poems, passing the book back and forth. The poetry seemed more like trim and elegant talking than "official poetry. It was more direct. We never did trust Wordsworth wandering off lonely as a cloud. Stafford's poetry seemed true to something, but we could not put a name to it. We liked it.

I must admit that I've always liked Wordsworth in the "clouds," but I've never been sure how long I could stay with him there. Weightlessness is foreign to most of us. I suppose that the first question that comes to mind when I consider Stafford's weight or directness is whether or not you think that it had something to do with being a Midwesterner, and more

specifically, a Kansan? Could his straightforwardness have something to do with no-frills Kansas?

DAY: Bill told me that his voice came from his mother's voice, the way she talked. We all come from someplace, and that means we come from the way our mothers' talk, or the friends we have, or the books and poets we read. And maybe it comes from where we live, but not in sense that we should become sentimental about it. Kansas is a fine, flat and profane place to live if you happen to be in White Woman Creek country. But if you are in Northeast Johnson County, I am not sure how much that differs from John Updike country. I would have been a different writer had I lived among the Cambridge Ladies, and e.e. cummings would have been a different poet had he been reared in Bly, Kansas. But after we observe the obvious, what have we said? My guess is it is more a matter of subject than of tradition and the individual talent. T.S. Eliot was from St. Louis and some of what he writes is Greek to me.

Can you give us an example of a few lines from Stafford that shows "his mother's voice"? I find this idea intriguing. But having heard this I wonder what then is regionalism? Does it exist in poetry and prose in the manner of painting and printmaking? If so, is this the "subject" of the verse, rather than the place ringing through?

DAY: I cannot because Bill did not. I think he was talking about how if you print out ten or twenty lines of his poetry and ask students (who have studied a number of 20th century American poets) whose poetry is this, they will say Stafford. Some writers have voice (I am told I have it), and some don't. Bill's point was that he didn't get it from Kansas; he got it from his mother. That said, I don't think you need voice to be a good writer. I never thought Katherine Ann Porter had voice, but she is among the finest prose writers we've ever had in America.

As to regionalism, it comes with being an American writer: Barth and Maryland; Cather and Wright Morris and Nebraska; Twain and Missouri; even Salinger and New York. Faulkner and Mississippi. Porter and Texas. The achievement is to make the singular something larger. Leslie Fiedler writes about this very

134

well toward the end of *Love and Death in the American Novel.*
And Barth, once in conversation with me, put it like this: "You
don't want to become the poet of West North Dakota." Many are
called. Very few are chosen. Bill Stafford was chosen. His poetry
has reach.

**I like your point about voice. I see that. What I'm getting at is
whether or not there was some connection between the land
and the poet that may have been different had he (Stafford)
been from a different place. Maybe his use of natural imagery,
for instance. I think there's a good deal of food for thought on
Stafford's statement that his voice came from his mother.**

DAY: Bill never believed voice came from terrain. He would
shake his head slightly no when the subject was broached. But it is
also true that what we writers describe (Updike's suburbs;
Salinger's Central Park; Bill's Western Kansas) does involve
terrain. It is what we see. We all would have told different stories
or written different poems had we come from very different places
than we did (the American suburbs may be the exception). I have
written stories set in France and stories set in the California, and
Bill has written poems set on college campuses and in the far
Northwest. We come from specific places (most of us), but we
move around; what probably doesn't change is the voice, and that
(I agree with Stafford) doesn't come with the territory.

**Okay. This makes sense. So voice aside, let's take a minute
then and talk about terrain as inspiration. Specifically, it
appears that you write heavily with the landscape of Kansas in
mind, as well as France when you were overseas. Do you think
writers find rejuvenation in "terrain," especially one that can
be called home? Would you say that Kansas recharges your
batteries?**

DAY: When you use description as part of setting, you naturally
use where you've set your stories. I wrote a novella called *In My
Stead,* which is set in both California and Kansas. When my
character looks around in California, he sees the plush suburb
where he lives; when he remembers Kansas (Wolf, Kansas—a
one-family town, the family being his), he sees the flat land of

High Plains. In another novella, *The Four Wheel Drive Quartet*, I set the story in both an East Coast college town and again in Western Kansas. I hope the reader senses that the narrator in both cases likes Kansas better than either California or the East Coast college town. But that is a matter of the character, not of his author (although I do prefer the High Plains over the suburbs of Southern California and the staid society of the East Coast—but I wouldn't want to choose Rue de Seine in Paris over West Dirt of Bly, Kansas. Both have their appeal.) But back to Bill Stafford: he once wrote a poem set in Garden City, Kansas, that had a blue Hudson in it. That's pretty specific in terms of both time and territory, but somehow it gets beyond both of those. I think it is not only his craft (which I suspect was largely a gift), but the way his poems become very subtle extended metaphors. Whole poems like "Near" become something more than they seem. In this case, a love poem. Very fine.

Well, this may be too large of a question to address in a few words, but do you see William Stafford in your work? For instance, maybe in a bit of advice he gave you, or in a work ethic which he employed? If so, can you speak on this?

DAY: Yes. Sometimes when I'm stuck I'll read his poetry to see how he fashioned his reticence. When I cut back my prose to what I hope is a clean line, I think that might have come from my reading of Bill. And in his best poems ("Weather Report" among them) he is just on the edge of sentimentality. But he doesn't go over. I've dared to approach that edge myself, but with I think less success in getting there and sometimes failing not to go over. His *Stories That Could Be True* (autographed with a picture of me he took inside) is always on my desk. As for the title: It speaks for what I try to accomplish.

If we may speak in terms of a legacy, what does William Stafford leave for poets, Kansan or otherwise?

DAY: I expect Bill is now out of fashion. We are all reading John Ashberry these days (a very fine poet but in a different way). Being out of fashion means that at some point if you are good enough (and Bill is), your work will finally weave itself into the fabric of American letters. I remember when we all had never heard of Jean Rhys (not American, I know), and now her two Paris novels and her short fiction are part of the literary cloth. I think Melville was out of print at one point. In any case, what Bill leaves is so good and strong that I am reminded of Philip Larkin's observation about such poetry, which went something like this: Don't ask, "What does it mean?" Just wonder, "My god, how did he do it?" That's what I wonder every time I read Bill's better poetry. "Alive, still, waiting to be born"—What a line [from "Traveling Through the Dark"]! Those commas around "still." The line a unit of attention just as William Carlos Williams defined a free verse line. How did he do it?

WILLIALM STAFFORD MEMORIAL POETRY RENDEZVOUS & OTHER WRITINGS

By Steven Hind

I.

It is easy to take poets for granted once they become official masters, consigned to the textbooks where obligation leads the way. Few poets resist that sort of assigned approval more vigorously than William Stafford. Certainly, he shows us a great deal about how language works, as poets should and as teachers demand, but beyond that, he shows us how an unpretentious skepticism is the hallmark of healthy intelligence, and if not conceived here, certainly at home on the Plains. It's not a political stance in any narrow sense, yet it speaks to the mindset that checks excess, political or otherwise

It's "Aunt Mabel" saying about the "Senator" who "talked war, "He's a brilliant man,/ But we didn't elect him that much." It's giving voice to the naked presumption of "Religion Back Home" where the insinuation too often is, "Our Father Who art in Heaven / can lick their Father Who art in Heaven." It's the homely dynamic of family in "Vacation Trip" as the speaker begins, "The loudest sound in our car/ was Mother being glum." It's the mild candor of "Freedom" asserting that "Most of the world are living by / creeds too odd, chancy, and habit forming/ to be worth arguing about by reason." It's the quiet profundity of a long night's drive in "Family Trip" "past the town where I was born," it's dividend: "Once you cross a land like that/ you own your face more." Even in his most extravagant moments he demonstrates my favorite remark about our native posture: "You Kansans, no hype allowed."

William Stafford's words are both good poetry and good medicine, antidote to the poisons of self-aggrandizement and its blurring of perception. He is a tonic for the mind.

If poets are guardians of our words, this poet is also a guardian of something more: a gentle courage that welcomes fellow seekers into the long ordeal of "getting used to being a person." As the poet Louis Simpson said of Stafford, "He is a poet of the people in the deepest and most meaningful sense."

II.[i]

I'll take my cue from Stafford's poem, "A Course in Creative Writing" that begins, "They want a wilderness with a map — / but how about errors that give a new start?" I like that dash, signaling the next thing that occurs to him.

I'm drawn to the way he faces truths, some of them not so laudable, without rancor, resentment, or self-righteousness. And that apposition in "Vocation," about the antithesis of father and mother, she calling "us back to the car:/she was afraid; she always blamed the place,/the time, anything my father planned." I think we recognize that dynamic, although for many it could be gender-reversed, but who else would state it with such neutrality, just recalling "the way it is"?

The synthesis of humility, humor, and clear-eyed perception that seems solidly Midwestern/Kansan, to me — it's everywhere in the poetry. There are poems that ride the line between wit and sobering assessments, as in "Purifying the Language of the Tribe" or the stunning "Thinking for Berky," with its "survivors in your beds/... so far and good." His sister-in-law told me she remembered that girl, in El Dorado. "He didn't even change her name," she said. On and on.

By the way, the "river under First and Main" he refers to in "Prairie Town" is now open with a park around it and a mural on the north-facing wall, with Bill Stafford sitting in the lower right-hand corner: Chalk one up for our side.[ii]

I didn't mean to catalog his work, but I suppose pulling them up like ducks in a shooting gallery at least illustrates how deeply I am influenced by him. I think that's true for a great many people. He answered letters from everyone. He made one feel taken into the embrace of his respect.

The instant recognition of so many of his standards and judgments pulled me into his orbit, of course. His personality seemed closer to his work than any other poet I've ever met, and a few of them seemed despicable as people. . . .

I guess I fluttered past his quiet utterances until I began teaching them. I suspect I always taught myself more than I taught anyone else. So, truth be told, I probably didn't connect right away. I think I had to grow into Stafford's poetry and his point of view.

I hated the Vietnam war, thought it a fool's errand from the get-go, but I had no tradition from which to resist the draft and was called up for induction even though I was married and teaching in Topeka. I rode up to Kansas City on the army bus with former students! The only reason I wasn't drafted was because I had a bone spur in my knee, which disqualified me.

Out here [Hutchinson], the first of my brilliant Mennonite students gave a speech (I had a double major in college and taught speech for a few years out here) on conscientious objectors. I soon found *Down in My Heart*, [iii] which pulled me into Bill's orbit at once. And I read some of Gerald Heard at Stafford's mention of him, of going to Heard's California ranch to talk about war resistance, etc. I suspect that Bill's courage of conviction was as attractive as his poetry, although they are of a single cloth.

Well, I looked back at the few letters I received from him. (I didn't write often because I had the half-conscious sense of intruding, of burdening an important man — how Kansan is that!) His letter of January 1978 mentions the Boulder encounter in his thank you for our hosting him here that winter. A letter in 1983 offers me his editor's name since I had mentioned writing a novel but having no sense of what to do with it. I see that on Kansas Day, 1988, I included "Religion Back Home" in a presentation to a women's group out here. From then on, I don't think I ever gave any sort of talk or presentation where I didn't include work by William Stafford. And *Writing the Australian Crawl* is among the most liberating books on writing I've ever read. In person, in his advice and counsel on writing, and in the spare, modest, and often witty brilliance of his work — Stafford raised the Plains voice, let us say, to a level of authentic expression that places him among the best of American voices. Or so I believe.

141

III. Stafford Poems by Steven Hind

A CHOSEN WAY
"... judge me: I came away." William Stafford, "Prairie Town"

This Bill of art and right paused at
a fence one day and saw prairie
dogs perched at their doors.

"Citizens," he heard the day saying
in its own strange way, "I grant
you rights to your town."

Then he turned back for the town
where he had slept the stretching
nights and cored the light in his way.

He followed to the river south of town
and felt the current in his fingers,
felt the trustworthy flow, baptizing
that hand chosen for life.[iv]

SUMMER NIGHT, TO BILL

On the road tonight under stars—
Milky Blur, I christen it, Bill—
traveling the dark with the trucks
and the skunks, I thought of you.
Near Abilene a stain passed under
my lights, apostrophe where some
deer met fate in confusion, and
your poem whispered again.
        At two,
past all disasters that did not happen
tonight, I squat in a bath of breezes
under my cottonwood where a thousand
leaves believe in summer, saying be
true. You are. Old traveler, adios.

142

THE MURAL AT FIRST & MAIN

We stood by the river that passes through our town
where the artist on sabbatical had painted a white
wall with stars, and the shouldered child, the Ferris
Wheel, and the little man in a low corner seeing it
all—He was the target of my gesture. "He is a great
poet and he lived in your town as a boy," I said
to the neighbor child of my afternoon's charge.
"See, he's seeing and writing it all down in the book
on his lap," I said. "You could read his books and . . ."
Then her phone rang, and she snapped open the device
and spoke to her chum, Gabby, the name an irony
too rich for all but coincidence. I followed her back
to the car, the device at her ear, the pair alive in their
brave new moment—while the little man in my brain:
"The poet's words, they could save your life."

---

[i] Kirsten Bosnak conducted an extensive, unpublished interview with
    Steven Hind in 2008. This is an excerpt.
[ii] The Arkansas River flows through Hutchinson. The mural was
    designed by Dave Loewenstein of Lawrence, Kansas.
[iii] Stafford's master's thesis at the University of Kansas, later published.
[iv] In a letter to the author, March 15, 2001.

NEW DOORS: LESSONS FROM BILL

By Ingrid Wendt

1) While not desirable, it is possible, given the lack of a table, to stand behind and write a poem atop the television on which your wife is watching the news.

It is Summer, 1975, and Bill and Dorothy Stafford, my husband Ralph Salisbury and I and our three year-old daughter are in Jackson Hole, Wyoming, all expenses paid by a Brigham Young University professor, Clinton Larson, who's hired Bill, Ralph, me, and novelist John Williams, plus various one-day guests, to teach in a two-week-long writing conference.

My inclusion on that faculty is pure good fortune. I am fresh from being a stay-at-home-Mom (before that term was invented), with an MFA and three years of teaching experience at the university level, and Clint knew a good deal when he saw one. We faculty don't yet know that Clint will run out of funds, failing to pay the promised wages to either Bill or myself (Ralph and John do get their checks, and, years later, Clint makes things right with Bill, too); but even had I known, I would have gladly, and even intentionally, forfeited wages for the chance to work side by side, several hours a day, in the windowless basement of a bank, with William Stafford, whose poems and ways of meeting the world have ever since been an inspiration to me.

Our daily sessions go like this: we read aloud and orchestrate group critiques on student poems, first thing each day. Bill talks about following our hunches, about noticing how our own words can take us along new trails, about giving ourselves permission to play with language and to enjoy the results. Bill has a phenomenal ability to make a point by calling up lines and points made by other writers, seldom claiming authority for himself. How I wish to know enough to do that, too! And then Bill and I take turns offering daily assignments, which everyone, ourselves included, works on and shares the next morning—which isn't easy for me, I silently complain, needing to wait till Martina is fast asleep before I can even *begin* to write, on the desk we are lucky enough to have in our good-

145

sized room.

And then, a week or so into the conference and just before supper, I knock on Bill and Dorothy's door, just down the motel balcony from ours. "Come in," one of them calls, and there is Bill, completing his assignment atop the TV, with Dorothy watching the news, both of them as calm as if this happened every day. And a second door, one I never suspected was there, opens, too, showing me a way of life I'd never imagined: a life in which the level of language and attentiveness, to which we poets aspire, need not depend on solitude or a visit from "the muse." Our "poet selves" can (imagine!) be present all day long, wherever we find ourselves, with others or alone. Here, in Jackson Hole, Wyoming, given Bill's example, I understand in a flash what I saw repeated over and over during the many years of our long friendship: that to each moment of each day, no matter where he was, Bill could bring a "breathing respect" for the gifts he knew he would find there. His "way" was, in a sense, to overlay the words of poetry on the template of "now," while fully engaged in both. It is a way I have aspired to, all my life. Once in a while, I come close.

Here is a poem, written August 26, 1993, two days before his death, which Ralph and I see every day in our kitchen:

You Reading This, Be Ready

Starting here, what do you want to remember?
How sunlight creeps along a shining floor?
What scent of old wood hovers, what softened
sound from outside fills the air?

Will you ever bring a better gift for the world
than the breathing respect that you carry
wherever you go right now? Are you waiting
for time to show you some better thoughts?

When you turn around, starting here, lift this
new glimpse that you found; carry into evening
all that you want from this day. This interval you spent
reading or hearing this, keep it for life –

What can anyone give you greater than now,
starting here, right in this room, when you turn around?

> (Reprinted from *The Way It Is: New & Selected Poems* by William Stafford, Graywolf Press, Saint Paul, Minnesota)

2) It's impossible to write a truly bad poem (especially if you're William Stafford).

Same summer, same conference. Bill's assignment one day: a contest to see who can, before morning, write the most terrible poem. It is not easy for any of us, and finding this out becomes a lesson to give heart to even the least experienced writers in our group; but I, who love competition, nearly despair. Worthy turns of phrase keep slipping in, and have to be excised; fresh images intrude, and have to be struck.

Nevertheless, by morning, guess who, ta-da, is the winner? My poem (which, regretfully, I have not kept) is full of clichés and sappy rhymes, on a subject so mundane I cannot, today, remember what it was. Bill, on the other hand, is the big time loser. <u>Big</u> time. What a fine poem he reads to us. Has he really done his best to be "bad?"   I think so. He says so. And what does that say to me, to us? Reader, I leave that up, in true Stafford fashion, to you.

3) If restaurant lights are too bright, and no one is looking, you can turn them down.

Flash backwards a few more years, to 1969, when I am a visiting/temporary assistant professor at a California institution of higher education, filling in for a poet who had just been fired by the school's administration for publicly extolling (off campus, but still…) the pleasures of marijuana. The Department of English has brought a civil suit against the administration (which they finally win); but someone else is needed to fill that poet's place until his case comes to court.

Enter the young, recent MFA graduate, me, who has not yet met National Book Award winner William Stafford, but who has the pleasure of taking him to visit her class for a reading, and later—with her soon-to-become-husband—out to dinner at a local steak house,

147

known for tasty food despite its tacky-vinyl, too-brightly-lit booths. Enter three poets, one of them famous, wanting a quiet spot for conversation. They head for the back room, just opened for the overflow, and to a booth as far as possible from Muzak and alcohol-inspired joviality. But it is still unbearably bright, each booth with its own blazing fixture on the wall above their heads. Two of them remark a bit, and apologize a bit, to their famous guest, who takes the proverbial bull by the horns, stands up, and –smiling slyly—reaches up inside the fixture and unscrews the bulb.

Ah! Such an unexpected rebellion, such a peaceful solution, with no one the wiser, except (on more than one level) Bill's hosts. Would I, all these years later, dare (as I always, unswervingly, do) ask a waitperson to kindly turn down the volume, or the lights (the do-it-yourself option usually not available) when either or both is too high? Maybe I would, by now; I've grown less timid. But certainly not – without Bill's example—at the age of 24.

"We poets are the pipsqueaks of the world," said Bill in 1982, under the dome of the Oregon state capitol building's rotunda, while accepting the Governor's Award for the Arts. Yes, yes, I nodded, we are. And still, as Bill's success in the world has shown, and to borrow from cliché, the squeaky wheel (sometimes) gets the grease.

4) "Who needs it?"

Fast forward from California in 1969, to Oregon in the early 1980s. I've been asked by the Oregon Arts Foundation to serve as a judge for that year's literary fellowships. The other two judges? Poet William Stafford and fiction writer Damon Knight. Several weeks before our meeting in Salem, each of us has received a packet of fiction and poetry by Oregon residents. It is a lot of reading, but I look forward to the discussions the three of us will have.

Troubling me, however (in those days, when this contest was not judged anonymously), is a group of poems by a young, up-and-coming poet who has had one book published by a well-known small press. I appreciated the poems in that book. I appreciate these new ones, too. Without *liking* them, I can admire their cleverness, their intelligence, their mastery of craft. But what are they about? Sad to admit, they say nothing to me, maybe (I fear) because I'm still young and inexperienced and not well-enough read. And, because the poet is also young and smart and well-known, I fervently wish to say something nice. Maybe we'll just have to let him win one of the fellowships.

Entry by entry, the three of us discuss, in the order in which their work was received, the ratings we've privately given each one. Happily, we seldom disagree. And then we get to the work by aforementioned locally-famous poet. Bill, taking the lead, asks what we think. Damon and I hesitate and swerve a bit, looking for careful words; but Bill doesn't wait. "Who needs it?" he asks. Bingo! Bravo! Turning those poems face down, we move on.

5) And one more, out of many others: Bill's way ("Smoke's Way") brings us together.

Fast-forward twenty-nine years to Oregon, again, where Ralph and I have lived since 1971, with time out for Fulbright appointments in Germany, and other travels, conferences, and brief periods of residence overseas. Our daughter is grown; she has graduated from the University of Oregon; she has lived and worked in Italy for several years; she is married, now, with a family of her own.

Bill Stafford has died. The news hit us hard, in August of 1993, as it hit all who knew and loved him. Ralph and I mourned, that August, together with many friends, at the memorial celebration of Bill's life, on the wide lawn of Lewis and Clark College, where he taught for many years. We also rejoiced in the enduring gift of his long friendship, and in the large community of writers and readers who were also his friends and who gather, now, several times a year under the umbrella of a non-profit organization, the Friends of William Stafford (FWS), with a working board of Oregon poets and readers of poetry, with an advisory board of many of our United States' poetry's "notables," and with members across the country and around the world.

Just this past week, we've attended a gathering in the home of FWS board member Paulann Petersen, herself a poet, to celebrate the 94th birthday of Dorothy Stafford, my adult life-long friend and role model of vivacity, kindness and grace, with an allegiance to the present so like that of her late husband. And I, this week, along with more than 56 volunteers across the country and overseas, am orchestrating in my city of Eugene, Oregon, for the tenth time and with the help of friends Martha and Jerry Gatchell, what other Stafford fans are planning in theirs: a community birthday celebration of the life and work of poet William Stafford. These January celebrations, with audiences made up of those who met Bill once or twice, or more, or not at all, take many forms. Some consist of panels of writers and readers, commenting on Stafford's poems. More often, they feature local writers of note, who read Stafford poems as well as their own. In ours, as well as in others, audience members are invited to read a favorite Stafford poem, along with one of their own, written in the spirit of Stafford's work. Each year, for more than ten years, Bill's readers have grown and grown in number and in devotion.

Our celebration this year will focus on Stafford's pacifism, a conviction he took from his Kansas upbringing and from parents who instilled in him compassion, independence of thought, and a love of justice (which will take "millions of intricate steps"). In his poem "Graduate," he wrote: "How kind we were to each other at home...." In "How My Mother Carried on Her Argument with the World," we find these words about learning to get on with others: "Your / expression studies theirs and becomes whatever / they need." And:

> You listen carefully, and never allow the hail
> of their multiple little blunders – or the vast
> arc of their wild misunderstandings – to register
> in your unswerving, considerate gaze.

This year, like other years, we will conclude our program with a documentary film about Bill and his work. We will see the most recent of several fine ones: Haydn Reiss's "Every War Has Two Losers," which takes its title from the posthumous book of Stafford's poems and journal entries drawn from a lifetime of pacifism, following time spent in work camps as a Conscientious Objector during World War II.

This year it's happened again: in my planning an event to honor Bill, and to bring new readers to his work, I am making new friends: the filmmaker, Californian Haydn Reiss, who has allowed us to use his DVD cover design as the template for our poster; his designer, Maryann Lipaj, who, in Ohio, designed our poster *pro bono*; several Facebook poets across the country, who saw my post about our Eugene event, with whom I've now exchanged books, letting them know (at their request) how they can, next year, sponsor celebrations of their own.

As Bill says at the end of Reiss's film, "Here's how to count the people ready to do right. One. One. One." They are everywhere around us. You, reader, I think you must be one.

Smoke

Smoke's way's a good way – find,
or be rebuffed and gone:
a day and a day, the whole world home.

Smoke? Into the mountains I guess
a long time ago. Once here, yes,
everywhere. Say anything? No.

I saw Smoke, slow traveler, reluctant
but sure. Hesitant sometimes, yes,
because that's the way things are.

Smoke never doubts though:
some new move will appear.
Wherever you are, there is another door.

William Stafford, published in *Smoke's Way*,
Graywolf Press, 1983

RUNNING TOWARD THUNDER

By William Sheldon

William Stafford's definition of a poem as "anything said in such a way or put on the page in such a way as to invite from the hearer or reader a certain kind of attention" serves, of course, as departure point for discussing Stafford's own poetry, effectively describing that experience for the reader: suddenly, amidst a welcoming voice, we are brought to the kind of attention that accompanies real epiphany, the sometimes frightening moment that makes us take account of the conduct of our lives.

Such an epiphany can be seen in what is probably Stafford's most widely known poem, "Traveling Through the Dark," in which the speaker finds "a deer / dead on the edge of the Wilson River road." Examining the deer, he discovers she is pregnant, her fawn "alive, still, never to be born." At the poem's end he states, "I thought hard for us all—my only swerving—, / then pushed her over the edge into the river." Initially desiring a kind of salvation for the fawn, many readers ultimately experience epiphany when they come to understand the vainglorious nature of such inclination. Or, as Stafford puts it in an interview with Steven Hind, "there are windows that open and close like steel traps," adding "so it was for the deer." His point is that we need to realize when a window is closed and choose to do something else, rather than to push at a window that is not only shut but no longer exists. He discussed how that realization is not good enough for some people, those who would perform drastic acts even after it is too late to effect change, stating that sort of mindset leads to terrorist acts that don't do any good but ease one's conscience. In the interview, Stafford says, "I don't want to ease my conscience; I want to do good." Sounds simple enough, right? Try living your life that way, even for one day.

That sentiment informs most, if not all, of Stafford's poetry, which is hard thinking in the service of doing good. Poetry of that sort is important in a time often at odds with such an approach, a time of ongoing war, when a hard idea like patriotism is dispensed with by the easy wearing of magnetic "ribbons" on the trunks of our cars going their ways on unrationed gas. Those ribbons, stating "We support our troops," ease our consciences without confronting the harder issues of the wars those troops are fighting. Stafford's poetry is welcome tonic to such slavish behavior. In "At the Un-National Monument along the Canadian Border," he begins, "This is the field where the battle did not happen, where the unknown soldier did not die" and ends discussing the place as "ground / hallowed by neglect and an air so tame / that people celebrate it by forgetting its name." The reader may chuckle at first but the realization comes quickly that what we value, what we turn to monument, may be terribly askew.

The poems in this volume take no less of a hard look at the world they define. However, being hard-eyed is not the same as being cynical. In the last stanza of "A Dream," the speaker states, "Anything we do can fail—I know that. In love, though, / there are millions of ways to fail: / all are sacred." Likewise, the last stanza of "One Home" states,

> The sun was over our town; it was like a blade.
> Kicking cottonwood leaves we ran toward storms.
> Wherever we looked the land would hold us up.

That world may have a hard edge to it, our sun like the sword of Damocles hanging above us, but it must be embraced, in the way of children running toward thunder (and its accompanying lightning), because it will sustain us.

Stafford, famous for returning student writing with his "noticings" rather than "praise" or "blame," in the same manner welcomes the local, the current, in his poetry, keeping himself open. And always behind Stafford's noticings, pulled from the current, is a strong sense of self-possession and a bountiful facility with language shaping ideas into something good, sharing and providing epiphanies. Those realizations are there for us, everyday, in the world, in these poems; we need only pay a certain kind of attention.

STAFFORD'S ALTERNATIVE WAY: QUIET REGARD

By Kirsten Bosnak

In *Early Morning*, Kim Stafford tells the story of one of his father's childhood encounters with injustice. On the playground, William Stafford sees two African-American children being taunted by others. "And what did you do, Billy?" his mother asks when he tells her about it after school. He answers, "I went and stood by them."[1]

Stafford was different from many poets and many people. He was gifted with a fierce regard for the disregarded. For him, empathy and listening were a matter of deep practice — a practice he articulates in his poetry, prose, and interviews. His way of calling out the most quiet voices is a relief, an alternative to the noise, competition, and attempts at domination we face daily in Western culture. In his introduction to *You Must Revise Your Life*, he writes, "Imposing my will on language — or on a student, or on the citizens of a country — was not my style."[2]

*

In April 2008, Kim Stafford came back to Kansas for a weeklong visit to read his father's poems, to give workshops, to see his Aunt Mar, who had married his father's younger brother. Kim and I talked for an hour one morning in the bunkhouse at the Flying J, a working ranch outside Cottonwood Falls. I had asked how he could account for his father's spiritual courage. But Kim, who is always ready with a thoughtful answer, was at a loss for words. Finally, shaking his head, he said, "There is no accounting for it," but he talked a little more about the playground story. The black children were new to the school; the taunting was their reception, but Billy Stafford, symbolically, stood with them. "Where did he get the notion that one should do that, *could* do that, that he personally could do that, no matter what happened?" Kim wondered out loud.[3] And I wonder, too.

William Stafford wasn't interested in popular people and had the courage to make unpopular choices. Kim told me that his father, at

155

gatherings like the one taking place that day at the ranch, would hang back from the center and seek out the people at the edges.

The same approach — regard for what goes unnoticed — is at work in Stafford's poetry. We see it in the collection of his early poems, *Another World Instead*[4], which had just come out in the shops the week I talked with Kim. Stafford wrote many of these poems during his years in Civilian Public Service camps, where he served as a conscientious objector during World War II (years that certainly gave him firsthand experience in being marginalized). They sketch out a portrait of a man with open eyes, open ears, and an open heart. Consider excerpts from two poems written in Los Prietos, California, within a nine-month period:

> An acorn falls on our roof in the night
> Pattering down to the eaves;
> We think our way through the quietness
> To the steadfast moon on the leaves.
> — From "Night Sound"[5]

> I heard the homeless laugh.
> I heard the prisoner sing.
> I knew I could not leave my place with them for anything.
> — From "Prison Camp"[6]

But Stafford goes beyond quiet attentiveness — again and again. *The Darkness Around Us Is Deep*[7], the collection edited by Robert Bly, offers a range of examples. Some poems call attention to the disregarded by presenting empathy or acts of regard, some by presenting acts of disregard.

In "Waiting in Line," Stafford's persona respects and relates to the elderly:

> I have glimpsed from within the gray-eyed look
> at those who push, and occasionally even I
> can achieve your beautiful, bleak perspective
> on the loud, inattentive, shoving boors
> jostling past you toward their doom.[8]

In "Listening," he honors the ability to notice small beings: "My father could hear a little animal step,/or a moth in the dark against a screen."[9] "At the Bomb Testing Site" sets a lizard, here representative of small, non-human beings, at the center of a supposedly human-centered world:

> It was looking at something farther off
> than people could see, an important scene
> acted in stone for little selves
> at the flute end of consequences.[10]

In "A Thanksgiving for My Father," the father speaks sympathetically of the prisoner and sees the warden's act as criminal; Stafford relates even to the wind in his regard for the prisoner:

> The freezing convict wanted
> back in prison. The warden
> laughed and let the storm execute
> him. The wind mourned.[11]

Stafford's famous poem "Serving with Gideon" shows an act of service — bringing a cup of Coca-Cola to the elevator man, marginalized because he is black.[12] "Remembering Brother Bob" expresses the speaker's (pretty clearly Stafford's) remorse at having been less sympathetic than possible, as an older child, toward his very young brother.[13] Finally, "Saying from the Northern Ice," shows respect for a most vulnerable non-human figure: "Over your shoulder is God; the dying deer sees Him."[14]

*

Stafford's writing says this kind of attentiveness must extend to everyday talk. Are we receptive listeners, or do we talk over others? Communication means true exchange; in a chapter titled "Workshop Insights," he writes, "Some people are so much in favor of free speech that they don't give you a chance to talk."[15] In the poem "At the Chairman's Housewarming," Stafford calls empty conversation "jelly talk" and likens it to a jellyfish that touches and spoils everything:

> The jelly talk stole out on the cloth

157

and coated the silver tine by tine,
folding meek spoons and the true knifeblades
and rolling a tentacle into the wine.[16]

"Jelly talk" infects the group and stops meaningful connection, ruining the gathering.
One of the most direct expressions of Stafford's thinking about the interconnectedness of receptive listening, intentional expression, and spiritual power comes in his essay "A Witness for Poetry":

My kind of assertion is to give individuals plenty of room in which to make their own decisions ... To me democracy isn't the process in which any group that is loud enough or rich enough can impose ideas on another group. Democracy is a situation in which we don't try to overwhelm each other ... Don't tell me what forensic speakers have forced on you. Relax, forget them. Tell me quietly, here in this room, what you really think. *The speaker who forces his thoughts on you is not cherishing your thoughts.* I value what you say. I'm using quiet forensics in my poems. The power of that, and its
great gain over the other kind, the loud kind, is that it incorporates those silences and gives each side a time to think. The silences are important ... [17]

*

Stafford practiced the same attentiveness in his teaching. "Those so-called confident people — they're quite vulnerable, too, and we find that out together," he said in an interview about workshops. "I feel an allegiance to the mildest, the timidest, the most tongue-tied."[18] His job as a teacher was "to *listen*, receive signals of all kinds," not "to foster an attitude of dominance" over students.[19] He discouraged competition, even with oneself, and waited for students to make "the first move."[20] Yet, he would find ways to get students to make that first move if he felt it would help them. In "The Classroom Contract" he writes about a student whose written work "galvanized" him (an example of his deft use of verbs) but who said not a word in class. Wanting to bring her into group conversation — but wanting the idea to come from her — he asked her near the end of a class meeting if she hadn't offered to begin a class discussion. He knew she hadn't, but his "maneuver" opened the way for her, and she volunteered. He sensed that she "was looking for an excuse to do it." [21]

Stafford was deeply conscious of the differences among individuals and was sensitive to their levels of readiness. He writes about this in "Workshop Insights," and though he is writing about his poetry, the same idea extends to conversation, teaching, or any kind of encounter. "I think what I'm trying to locate is that condition of a being who has not been distorted from the receptive, accurate encounter with experience," he says in an interview. "It's possible to overlearn fear or overlearn confidence." [22]

*

Years after his death, Stafford helps me learn confidence in the value of my own quietness, vulnerability, and sensitivity, to see them as blessings. He affirms the importance of listening and noticing over fitting in. He helps me have the courage to give voice to my regard for the marginalized. Maybe, with practice, this can strengthen the poems I write. Maybe they, like Stafford's, will help someone someday.

William Stafford also reminds me that it sometimes is futile to try to engage with those who use forceful language or who talk "jelly talk." He has helped me become more adept at excusing myself or changing the subject when I talk with someone who evidently does not cherish my (or others') thoughts. When we attend to and call out the quiet voices, we gain valuable information. We learn about ourselves. When we practice this attitude, we embrace the way of consensus, the way of the peacemaker, the way toward balance. Such practice may save the earth.

[1] Kim Stafford, *Early Morning: Remembering My Father, William Stafford* (St. Paul, Minnesota: Graywolf Press, 2003) 39.

[2] William Stafford, *You Must Revise Your Life* (Ann Arbor: The University of Michigan Press, 1986) 21.

[3] Kim Stafford, "The Poet Father, the Poet Son," interview with Kirsten Bosnak, *Flint Hills Review*, Fall 2009.

[4] William Stafford, *Another World Instead: The Early Poems of William Stafford, 1937-1947,* edited with an introduction by Fred Marchant (St. Paul, Minnesota: Graywolf Press, 2008).

[5] Ibid. 33.

[6] Ibid. 43.

[7] William Stafford, *The Darkness Around Us is Deep: Selected Poems of William Stafford*, edited with an introduction by Robert Bly (New York: HarperCollins
Publishers Inc., 1993).

[8] Ibid. 34.

[9] Ibid. 74.

[10] Ibid. 110.

[11] Ibid. 75.

[12] Ibid. 87.

[13] Ibid. 97.

[14] Ibid. 131.

[15] William Stafford, from *The Answers Are Inside the Mountains: Meditations on the Writing Life*, eds. Paul Merchant and Vincent Wixon (Ann Arbor: The University of Michigan Press, 2003) 82.
This is one of the recent compilations of Stafford's prose.

[16] William Stafford, *The Way It Is: New & Selected Poems* (St. Paul, Minnesota: Graywolf Press, 1998) 113.

[17] William Stafford, "A Witness for Poetry," in *You Must Revise Your Life*, 60-61 (emphasis mine), originally "A Poet Responds," in *Oregon Historical Quarterly* 81, no. 2, Summer 1980.

[18] William Stafford, "An Allegiance to the Most Tongue-Tied," in The Answers Are Inside the Mountains, 66, originally an interview with Claire Cooperstein, *Poets and Writers Magazine*, March/April 1990.

[19] William Stafford, "Meeting the Workshop," 57 (emphasis Stafford's) and "Workshop Insights," 79 in *The Answers Are Inside the Mountains*.

[20] William Stafford, "Some Suggestions from Experience," in *The Answers Are Inside the Mountains*, 50, originally "He Renders to God," interview with Mike Archbold, *101—Coast Magazine of the Arts*, Autumn 1974; "The Minuet," in *Answers*, 59.

[21] William Stafford, "The Classroom Contract," in *The Answers Are Inside the Mountains,* 86-87.

[22] William Stafford, "Facing Up to the Job," in *You Must Revise Your Life*, 79, originally "William Stafford: An Interview with Nancy Bunge," *American Poetry Review* 10, no. 6, November/December 1981.

ON SWERVING:
THE WAY OF WILLIAM STAFFORD

By Robert Stewart

When William Stafford—a passivist, a registered conscientious objector during World War II — remembers his boyhood in Kansas, as he does in an essay called "William Stafford, 1914-," he describes one moment with a special reverence: "The first, great aesthetic experience I remember with my parents," he says, "was one weekend when my father brought home a shotgun, the blue barrel, the shiny walnut stock: I stood admiring the gun where it stood in the corner."

It is one thing for a boy to love a gun that much, but Stafford wrote that memoir as an older man, poetry's gentle soul. In a poem called "Evening News," from *Allegiances* (1970), he celebrates, more typically, the spiritual quality of nature:

In the yard I pray birds,
wind, unscheduled grass,
that they please help to make
everything go deep again.

Try to imagine this poet rising up from a duck blind to blast ducks out of the air. If there is a contradiction here, it is absorbed into who William Stafford was as a writer; it is absorbed into the life of writing itself. "Everything excited me," Stafford says when he describes going on those duck-hunting trips with his father, "the dark, the cool air, the steady car. . . . North of us was Great Bend, and around there Cheyenne Bottoms. On west was the salt marsh. Teal would be coming in, canvasbacks, buffleheads." His excitement shows up in the quality of his language. The proper nouns. The names. In literary work, general and abstract language usually signal that the writer has not achieved sufficient excitement for his subject.

The way of William Stafford starts with excitement, as a spiritual way of engaging with the world. The approach values discovery over certainty, wonder over wanting. I once wrote in the margin of a book by the translator and spiritual writer Stephen Mitchell, "Poetry teaches by example." I don't know if I stole the sentence or made it up, but here is what I think it means: Do not do what a poem says; do what a poem does. Do not live as a painting depicts life; live as the painting lives. Stafford's poetry extends our perceptions outward, toward a condition of reverence. The poet personifies, stylistically, John Keats' famous "chameleon poet," shedding his own identity and ideology for a particular, mostly direct response to his subject matter. Stafford revealed some of this approach in the early 1980s when a professor at Brigham Young University asked him, "Do you have a firm belief about the nature of God?"

"My sense of the nature of God," Stafford replied, "is neither firm nor infirm; it is just there." That sounds at first like a politician's answer; but it is a writer's answer. The inner life of writing is neither firm nor infirm. It wobbles in the wind. It goes where the river goes. Poet and Nobel Prize Laureate in chemistry Roald Hoffmann reframed the position in a 2006 essay. For him, faith does not lie on one side or another side but in the middle. "The middle is not static," Hoffmann writes, "my psychological middle as well as the chemical equilibrium. I like that. Yes, of course I also want stability. But I believe that extreme positions—the things you start out with in a chemical reaction, the things you finish with (all people A, bad, all people B, good; no taxes at all, taxed to death)—all of these are impractical, unnatural, boring."

How are we to understand the virtues of instability, something William Stafford seems to have grasped? I found a clue to this dilemma in 2005, by preparing a lecture on seventeenth-century Chinese Taoist paintings for Kansas City's Nelson-Atkins Museum of Art. Until the day I was invited to speak, just a few weeks earlier, I knew nothing about the subject. To have no firm beliefs on the subject could mean that I had been given an opening, and I took it. People in Kansas City might remember the example of jazz legend Charlie Parker, who moved out of the geographic middle, Kansas City, to a psychological middle, in New York, about 1938. He took a job washing dishes at Jimmy's Chicken Shack — placing himself, musically, neither inside nor outside, exactly where he wanted to be — solely because one night a week Parker could hear Art Tatum play piano.

The Tao teaches us humility as we seek our place in the order and harmony of the cosmos. There is a relationship established here. To go with "the way," the Tao, has been termed in Chinese as *wu wei*, sometimes translated "actionless activity." Neither active nor inactive. This is the eternal principle of seeking oneness with all that exists. "Like any other sustained human endeavor," William Stafford once said, "writing is best done in a condition of humility and welcoming of what comes."

We know that William Stafford had firm beliefs. Stafford rejected "action" in World War II by accepting action as a conscientious objector. He spent 1942 to 1946 in work camps in Arkansas, California, and Illinois, paid $2.50 per month to fight fires, plant trees, and build roads. In 1944 while in California, he met and married Dorothy Frantz, the daughter of a minister of the Church of the Brethren. Despite all those things, we aren't to get his values confused with what his poems can teach us. "The other source of my unrest," he once told an interviewer, "is that the whole validity of poetry is based on something other than just the shoveling in of content: poetry is an experience."

As a writer, a poet, myself, I approach the work of artists such as William Stafford almost as if I were a highway robber, a bandit, rummaging around in the pockets of what they have to say for inspiration and ideas I can use. *Give it to me*, I think. I am looking for something to sustain me. So, I look into his poem "Remembering Brother Bob," from *A Glass Face in the Rain*, 1982, and I ask what example this poem sets for me.

The speaker of the poem, age twelve at the time, had brought his brother, seven, to a frozen pond to play hockey, and the poem quickly asks us to look at what actually happened, to look at what is present:

The sun went down. I turned
and Bob was crying on the shore.

The center strophe, which follows those lines, pushes the stakes and says, like Socrates, that the unexamined life is not worth living.

Do I remember kindness? Did I
shield my brother, comfort him?

This poem sets the example for me of healthy uncertainty, self-examination, which leads to the acceptance of responsibility:

Yes, I carried him. I took
him home. But I complained. . . .

"You said you would be brave," I chided
him. "I'll not take you again."

William Stafford, as a teacher, followed a principle he called "no praise, no blame," in which all issues are in the particulars. Like the scientist Roald Hoffmann, we could say that misjudgments, moments of weakness, bursts of anger, all become part of a process that allows us to seek equilibrium. Stafford ends this poem by returning to observed fact, but this time, the facts carry more weight. No praise, no blame. The speaker is neither victim nor villain, but someone who accepts fully the range of his actions.

> Years, I look at the white across
> this page and think: I never did.

I remember the first time I met William Stafford in person, back in the late 1970s, when he read his poems in Kansas City. He probably was sixty-four or sixty-five years old at the time, and after he finished reading, a girl about ten years old raised her hand. "Mr. Stafford," she said, "when did you become a poet?"

His reply is one of the things that has sustained me many times over the years whenever I find the need to examine my own life as a writer. In retrospect, the more I learned about the man, the more his statement seemed to fit him. "Whenever anyone asks that," he said, "I always like to turn the question around and ask the adults in the room: 'When did you stop being a poet?'"

I think his answer was not as glib as it sounds at first. I don't think he meant that adults simply get too busy running errands and making a living. I think he meant something else that happens to adults. We become cynics. We become fixed. We stop believing in small moments and the glory of the world and start believing in our own conclusions about the way things are, or should be. It's true that the creative process most writers practice turns, at some point, from initial glee toward a grown-up intellect to help shape the work; but William Stafford's primary drive valued enthusiasm and receptivity over ideas and intellectual control. His desire for heightened experience, in his words, "an always-arriving present," gets to the heart of why people turn to poetry at all. What stands out for me in the story of his boyhood, above, is the phrase "Everything excited me." Listen to his further description of those hunting trips: "At first light, long scarfs of ducks came in, talking to each other as they dropped. The seething cattails and grasses whispered and gushed in the shadows. And the river was there, going on westward, past islands, along groves, into the wilderness, an endless world for exploring."

As a writer, myself, I struggle to achieve that purity of expression. I easily drift into philosophic statements designed mainly to show how smart I think I am. The inner life of writing requires discipline; as the Zen scholar R.H. Blythe has written, "If you do not put yourself in the way and block the view, everything appears as it is." I find that enormously helpful in understanding the example William Stafford set for us. His was a struggle, not always easy or given, to love the world as it is. The media culture today — interactive, global — gives all of us the opportunity to offer grand or earth-shattering opinions on living wills, the NFL draft, or the Pope. Everyone seems to lead off with a firm belief.

A poetry student of mine recently started a poem, "Morning is worthless— / vomiting me from the warmth of my blanket." What example do those lines set for us? We see that the poem isn't interested in the morning at all but in offering an opinion about the morning. My job as a teacher extends into showing how the writer can leave open opportunities for self-questioning and take responsibility for how she experiences morning. Here are two lines about morning from Stafford's poem "Put These in Your Pipe":

I walk out and stand in a clearing
while the snow falls all around.

See what I mean? William Stafford's directness and emotional restraint often sound like the seventeenth-century Chinese Taoist poet who said, "In the ninth month of the xinyou year (1621) on the road to Mount Hui, I described what I saw and added a picture of it." William Stafford could have written that and, in some ways, did in the opening of a poem about writing called "Every Morning All Over Again," from *You Must Revise Your Life*, 1986:

Only the world guides me.
Weather pushes, or when it entices
I follow. Some kind of magnetism
turns me when I am walking
in the woods with no intentions.

As philosopher Simone Weil has said, "Absolute unmixed attention is prayer." The crazy logic here is that the poetic miracle lives in

165

acceptance of the world, the thing itself, not in our interpretation of it. "The satisfaction of the hunger, the final justification of experience," scholar Helen White has said, "is to be found in the experience itself. . . . The contemplation of the object and not its conquest or use toward some other end, that is the purpose."

Because of such principles, one of William Stafford's best-known poems, "At the Bomb Testing Site," has always seemed to me uncharacteristic of the poet and unconvincing, exactly because he uses an object — a lizard in the desert — toward *some other end*. A poor panting lizard has been given the task of putting forward the poet's anti-war sentiment. I like the sentiment in that poem, what it says, but I am not convinced by what the poem does. "At noon in the desert, a painting lizard / waited for history," the poem tells us, and the final image has that lizard with "hands gripped hard on the desert." By suggesting that the lizard has any concept of history, and by using the word "hands" instead of "claws," the poet, in this poem, has overridden the demands of poetry. The poem has too much certainty. It never swerves. It has designs on us.

Could we say the above poem stumbles by being too sure of itself? At his best and most characteristic, William Stafford finds the energized middle, its room to swerve. I am stretching it, perhaps, to project Stafford as a Chinese Taoist poet, but the struggle of a human being to illustrate our connection to the harmonious oneness of the universe resonates in that way. "My most impressive [religious] experience I recall," he told the Brigham Young interviewer, "was on the banks of the Cimarron River in western Kansas one mild summer evening, when sky, air, birdcalls, and the setting sun combined to expand the universe for me and to give me the feeling of being sustained, cherished, included in a great, reverent story."

His poems teach us that we struggle to say even one honest thing. In the process, Stafford always risked being thought of as too plainspoken, sometimes even simple. With nice poetic justice, Stafford's poem called "Thinking about Being Called Simple by a Critic" is one of his greatest for showing us the way, the Tao, to a healthy inner life. The poem begins, "I wanted the plums, but I waited," which cannot be read without acknowledging the famous poem by William Carlos Williams "This Is Just to Say," which begins,

I have eaten
the plums

166

that were in
the icebox

Stafford and Williams share a common tradition. They both value colloquial diction, direct statement, imagery. So Stafford's use of plums here serves to gather a little moral support for himself in confronting the critic; and the allusion helps him regain his humor through acceptance of the world as it is, even the world of nasty critics. This is a poem about writing without saying so. The poet says he waited. He thanks the critic for his or her honesty. The poet simplifies his life. He lets the plums be plums. He practices humility with a joke on himself — opening the fridge, he says, "Sure enough the light was on."

This poem illustrates two bits of ancient wisdom I give my own students when I teach writing; both statements say the same thing. The first is a proverb from the Chinese: "The way is not difficult, but you must avoid choosing." The idea here, as Stafford shows us in the poem about the critic, is that writers, at their best, come to see things as they are, often right in front of their eyes.

In the dark with the truth
I began the sentence of my life
and found it so simple there was no way
back into qualifying my thoughts.

The second bit of wisdom is a proverb from the Italian-American philosopher Yogi Berra: "When you come to a fork in the road, take it." Yogi Berra claims he meant that literally — the road to his house forked, and both directions arrived at the same place — a fact that enhances the point William Stafford loved to make about writing: Don't be stopped.

I don't want to mythologize William Stafford into super-poet. He could be, as I said, heavy handed in his meaning. He often could be shaken, confused. I admire all of that because, in spite of his doubts, he would not be stopped. "Commitment is healthiest," wrote the philosopher Rollo May, "when it is not without doubt but in spite of it."

In what clearly is Stafford's most famous poem, "Traveling through the Dark" (1962), the speaker comes across that famous deer dead on the edge of the Wilson River Road, and, in the process of deciding the best course of action, the man decides to push it over the

167

cliff. Stafford uses the word "swerve" twice in that poem, once near the beginning and once near the end. Anytime a poet uses the same word twice in a poem, especially once near the beginning and once near the end, it's a big deal. It matters. Early in the poem, the speaker knows he has to get the deer off the road and says, "to swerve might make more dead." And toward the end, just before pushing the deer and its unborn fawn — still alive, waiting to be born—into the ravine, the speaker says, "I thought hard for us all — my only swerving —."

"Don't swerve," any driving instructor or parent would tell you. They likely won't tell you that spiritual life, just as the life of writing, demands that we accept our lack of certitude. "The man protective of his life will lose it," Jesus says in Matthew, "but the one casting life away on my account will preserve it." Over and over, great writing presents us with a condition of doubt, uncertainty, before it regains its equilibrium. This is the process, set as experience in the poem or story, of self-questioning: a spiritual zigzagging. Call it suspense, the structural component not only present but necessary in literary art. Some years after "Traveling through the Dark," William Stafford wrote a little poem called "The Swerve," in *Someday, Maybe*, 1973, which was his way of saying, let's have another look at this problem:

THE SWERVE

Halfway across a bridge one night
my father's car went blind. He guided
it on by no star but a light he kept in mind.

Halfway to here, my father died.
He looked at me. He closed his eyes.
The world stayed still. Today I hold in mind

The things he said, my children's lives—
any light. Oh, any light.

The question is, where do we find the light, any light? It's the light of the icebox, the gleam of the shotgun barrel, the sun. It shimmers, glows, and burns in front of you – in the people you meet, the neighborhood you walk. Still, we want examples. Antoine de Saint Exupéry, in a memoir called "The Craft," about flying over the Sahara Desert in the early days of aviation, reports how he and his radio operator became desperately lost at night among clouds. "With

168

sinking hearts," says Exupéry, "Neri and I leaned out, he on his side and I on mine, to see if anything, anything at all, was distinguishable in the void." Sound familiar? What they wanted was a beacon, and each time a star showed itself ahead. "Despite our dwindling fuel," Exupéry says, "we continued to nibble at the golden bait, which each time seemed more surely the true light of a beacon, was each time a promise of landing and of life – and we had each time to change our star."

The art and craft of writing is full of paradoxes. For Stafford, the process of writing, he said many times, was easy. "To get started, I will accept anything that occurs to me." Henry Miller said, "To begin, I begin anywhere." When you come to a fork in the road, take it. There is no sense in agonizing over the source of the next poem. If moonglow opens your way, go. A star. A beacon. "Any light. Oh, any light."

For Exupéry, over the Sahara, the stars led, eventually, to port at Cisneros. Later, Exupéry fictionalized the experience in *Night Flight*, with the pilot Fabien and his operator lost over the Andes Mountains and no choice at all but one. Unable to descend into the snowy mountains, they rose toward the stars. "Like plunderers of fabled cities [the fliers] seemed, immured in treasure vaults whence there is no escape. Amongst these frozen jewels they were wandering, rich beyond all dreams, but doomed."

If you seek a philosophic answer, fortune, wide acceptance, you lose both the light and the calling. The purpose of the writing life is to write. That's the central paradox of my own life as a writer: I work best when I am content, and to work, I must shake myself out of contentment. One writer friend, a journalist, pointed out once, "If it ain't hard, it ain't writing." To shake myself up, I have traveled, alone, to Central and South America, getting out of my small dusty room. William Stafford, it seems, lived his whole life in that childlike moment where "Everything excited me." To invoke the poet William Blake, "Energy is eternal delight." Whatever it takes, I have to strain harder to put myself into a state of uncertainty, where everything I come upon, like a tree full of parrots outside my window, becomes miraculous.

The quality of being excited by what the world gives us always has been, for me, the first position of most true writers. Henry Miller tells the story of a friend he met in Greece, a natural raconteur by the name of Katsimbalis, who could rhapsodize on nearly any small detail or thing. "It might be nothing more than that he had picked a flower by the roadside on his way home," Miller writes in *The Colossus of Maroussi*. "But when he had done with the story, that flower, humble though it might be, would become the most wonderful flower that ever a man had picked. . . . It would be known forever in the mind of the listener as the flower that Katsimbalis had picked."

"Feeling is first," said e. e. cummings, yet few writers paid more attention to craft and syntax. I concede — with cummings, Katsimbalis, Stafford — to glee and enthusiasm; but a discussion of any writer's work also demands that we speak up for the intellect. Another William, William Wordsworth, points out in his preface to the 1801 edition of *Lyrical Ballads* that, while we need the spontaneous overflow of powerful feelings, "poems to which any value can be attached were never produced on any variety of subjects but by a [writer] who, being possessed of more than usual organic sensibility, had also thought long and deeply." There are subjects given to us as writers that have more or less profound implications, such as that deer dead on the road, but something beyond subject lures us back to read about them many times. That effect usually tells us that the poet's intellect was at work, choosing language just so. William Stafford does not begin his poem with these lines:

> Driving at night, I came upon a dead deer
> on the shoulder of the Wilson River Road.

He writes,

> Traveling through the dark I found a deer
> dead on the edge of the Wilson River Road.

Words chosen *just so* distinguish a poem from an event. "Traveling through the dark" has resonance that "driving at night" does not, even though "driving" is more colloquial; and the word "edge" of the road connotes a potential, perhaps cosmic catastrophe that the word "shoulder" does not. The deer, here, is Katsimbalis' flower, is the stock of the shotgun, is the grove and the cattails. The deer doesn't matter. What matters is the poet's interior struggle, his uncertainty in the situation, his confrontation with the cosmic scheme. That's the Tao of William Stafford — while he was a passivist, he was not passive.

The poetic life puts us in danger. Stafford's art establishes his affinity with pioneer aviators, ascetics, mountain climbers. "Here I am at 17,000 feet, in desperate need of air," writes Peter Matthiessen in *The Snow Leopard*, the journal of his hike through the Tibetan plateau. The story of every great artist is the story of restrictions, of fuel, of room, of air to breath. Matthiessen might have had supper in a cave, huddled close to a small fire where elements seem to conspire against living. His battle — on foot, sleeping on ice, and cursing "the thrift that brought us, so to speak, to this pretty pass" — is for him to remain part of the conscious and living world. It's as though faith, itself, were in our own hands.

"The wind had come and / emptied our trail," William Stafford writes in "Kinds of Winter," from *Writing the Australian Crawl*, "back of us, ahead of us." How is it that hardship results in beauty, and a love of the world? Stafford's answer lies in the poem's tone, almost celebratory in its acceptance: "We looked at each other. Our winter had come." To have found his place, for but for that moment, is enough. For Matthiessen, it seems, the less apparent his comforts, the greater his joy. "I wonder why," he writes, "in this oppressive place, I feel so full of well-being."

For Matthiessen, the answer almost always appears that he does it himself; he stops taking in and starts giving out, measuring those small, domestic attentions against the peaks that rise everywhere around. "I wax my boots, I wash my socks," he records. Almost unacknowledged through it all, he could have written, "I write my book." William Stafford awoke early every day and followed the lead of what occurred to him, with discipline and determination. On the day of his death, Aug. 28, 1993, he left a poem called "Are You Mr. William Stafford?" which includes these lines:

> You can't tell when strange things with meaning
> will happen. I'm [still] here writing it down
> just the way it was. "You don't have to
> prove anything," my mother said. "Just be ready
> for what God sends." I listen and put my hand
> out in the sun again. It was all easy.

We like to think that art comes of hardship, that suffering and anger have their payoff, that every roach crawling across our cell carries on its back an inspirational glow. Art comes from taking out the trash, from washing the floor, from sweeping up. *It was all easy.* If the path swerves, we take it. What is it we allow? Grace. We allow ourselves to say yes.

171

Blyth, R.H. *Zen in English Literature and the Oriental Classics.* Tokyo: The Hokuseido Press, 1942.

Hoffmann, Roald. "The Tense Middle." National Public Radio: Morning Edition, July 3, 2006 http://www.npr.org/templates/story/story.php?storyId=5519776.

May, Rollo. *The Courage to Create.* New York: Norton, 1975.

Matthiessen, Peter. *The Snow Leopard.* New York: Penguin, 1987.

Miller, Henry. *The Colossus of Maroussi.* New York: New Directions, 1941.

Saint Exupéry, Antoine de. *Night Flight.* New York: Harcourt Brace Jovanovich, 1932.

—. *Wind, Sand and Stars.* New York: Harcourt Brace Jovanovich, 1939.

Stafford, William. *Allegiances.* New York: Harper and Row, 1970.

—. *You Must Revise Your Life.* Ann Arbor: University of Michigan Press, 1986

—. *The Way It Is: New & Selected Poems.* St. Paul: Graywolf Press, 1998.

—. *Writing the Australian Crawl.* Ann Arbor: University of Michigan Press, 1978.

Tide of Chaos, Fervor Within: Chinese Painters of the 17th Century Respond to Dynastic Upheaval. Nelson-Atkins Museum of Art, Kansas City.

White, Helen C. *The Metaphysical Poets: A Study in Religious Experience.* New York: The Macmillan Co., 1936.

Williams, William Carlos. *The William Carlos Williams Reader.* New York: New Directions, 1969.

MEETING WILLIAM STAFFORD

By Fred Whitehead

The room in the Kansas Union that night was packed with a couple of hundred people. He fished a handful of poems out of his pocket and read them, pausing to recall a respected professor, John Ise of the Department of Economics, and to mention that, actually, he had been "run out" of the State—an allusion to his position as a conscientious objector during World War II.

Afterwards there was an informal reception at Ed Ruhe's apartment. Some graduate students clustered around him, and went on and on about who might be up for this or that award. Frustrated and resentful of this line of talk, I rudely interrupted and blurted out: "I just want to say hello from a Pratt poet to a Hutchinson poet." He brightened up, and replied with a broad smile: "I used to go fishing on the Ninnescah River!" I cannot exactly speak for him, but my impression was that we were both glad to get away from the gossip about awards, and share something about the real world "out there."

Another time he gave a talk for a class at the University of Missouri in Kansas City. It was about poetry, how he wrote. He must have given this talk hundreds of times, but it seemed fresh and clear. A poem might start from anywhere, sort of creeping up or appearing with some small unexpected image or thought, and grow from there. I was reminded of what E. M. Forster once wrote about history, that instead of the steady march of progress, it could go sideways, like a crab. Or as Bill Stafford could have said, a crawdad on the bed of the Ninnescah.

MY SECRET FRIEND AND ME

By Caryn Mirriam-Goldberg

William Stafford is my secret friend and teacher. No matter that he hardly knew me — we only had a few short conversations with him when, in the 1980s, he graciously visited with Kansas poets, even young ones like me. No matter that he died in 1993, or that he spent most of his time half a continent away from me in Oregon. We didn't ever friend each other on Facebook, but still, he has been as steady a voice guiding me in my writing life as any living friend. There is even an organization now called "Friends of William Stafford," so there! I am not the only one.

I began pal-ing around with Stafford sometime in the early 1980s when I bought his book *A Glass Face in the Rain,* and shortly after that, *Stories That Could Be True.* He did not engage me at first hello, but rather at "Yellow Flowers," in which he writes of dying while seeing a yellow flower by the road while his pulse tells him, "'Come back, come back, come back'" and he concludes:

> . . . World with your flower, your candle —
> we flicker and bend; we hear wheels
> on the road — any sight, any sound — that music
> the soul takes and makes it its own. (*Glass Face in the Rain* 103)

Stafford shows me here how our bodies call to us, and we call to the world, and most of all, how our lives give us long-unfolding of what we are.

Stafford guides me as a writer when it comes to his quiet turns of language, his spare and precise images, his direct and earnest voice, but mostly he guides me as a human. In fact, I find much of his poetry speaks to our greatest question: how to live. Stafford asks and answers this question without pretension or overreach, false humility or flashy desperation. Instead, he journeys off the map of what is expected from us by culture, community, family and ourselves, and returns with love letters to the earth, little refrains of praise for the infinite expansiveness of the life force, and telegrams that call out, "Stop. Come home. All is forgiven."

In his poem "Assurance," he tells us, "You turn your head —/ that's what the silence meant: *you're not alone./* The whole wide

175

world rains down" (*Early Morning* 13). In "From Our Balloon Over the Providences," he concludes by telling us that the world, which does not care who we are, ". . . *reaches us millions of ways:/ little fireflies quiet as truth/ climbing their invisible trellis of dark*" (*Glass Face* 117).

He merged his advice for writing and living in his four superb books on writing –*Writing the Australian Crawl, The Answers Are Inside the Mountains, Crossing Unmarked Snow* and *You Must Revise Your Life*—all a combination of advice, interviews, considerations, questions. Here he gives me the best advice I've ever heard about writing: "Language can do what it can't say" *(Crossing Unmarked Snow* 6) and the best advice I have ever heard about living: "Treat the world as if it really existed (*Writing the Australian Crawl* 50). He also defines poetry in the same way one could explain spirit: it is what you "have to see from the corner of your life," without being too ill—or well-prepared. He goes on further: "A poem is a serious joke, a truth that has learned *jujitsu*. Anyone who breathes is in the rhythm business; anyone who is alive is caught up in the imminences, the doubts mixed with the triumphant certainty, of poetry" (*Writing the Australian Crawl* 3). Each time I read this quotation, I breathe a little more slowly.

When I read Stafford's poetry, I feel landed all over again in my adopted home of Kansas: in his words, I better understand the big sky and wide land. The rhythms of the juncos returning to the bird feeder outside my window on this icy day, the wind that will lift the blossoms of the redbud months from now, the storm that came with its panorama of lighting last summer—all this speaks through my not-so-secret friend. And what I want to say most to him now is this: Thank you, Friend, for giving me the world to which I've been given. Thank you for showing me how vast and deep is the blank page.

TALKING TO STAFFORD LATE AT NIGHT

By Caryn Mirriam-Goldberg

Never mind that you're a morning person or 18 years dead—
I hear you over my left shoulder. "Maybe," you say,
then nod. Outside, the pink sky has dissolved to black.
The snow exhales. Temperatures drop. The waning moon climbs
over the cusp of exhausted cedars. Juncos, chickadees and occasional
branches of sadness sleep. "Maybe what?" I ask,
keeping my hand moving on the window of the page.

Outside, you see what you always saw: dark on dark,
a glimmer of movement, a low call from where
the air glitters into itself. Behind the curtain of winter, spring.
Inside spring, lilac, hard to imagine. Yet the dirt
still manages to inhale the sky and make itself porous.
We wait together for me to find what I'm looking for.
Not something known and lost but the opposite. My hands
breathe. The steady almost undetectable buzz of everything
sings toward the wide arms of the dark horizon.

World, I could say if I were you, or Friend,
what would you have me do so that the perfect music
could come out, juxtaposing dark and home, song and field,
abandoned house of the heart and noiseless crowd of tall grass?
You wait in the dark, showing me time itself turns on "maybe,"
the "no" of what we cannot bear, the "yes" of all that is.

THE EARTH SAYS HAVE A PLACE: WILLIAM STAFFORD AND A *PLACE* OF LANGUAGE

By Thomas Fox Averill

In the Spring of 1986, my daughter was almost four years old and my wife and I were to have poet William Stafford to dinner during a visit he made to Washburn University. I searched for a short Stafford poem our daughter might memorize as a welcome and a tribute. We came across this simple gem, and she spoke it to him at the table.

Note

Straw, feathers, dust—
little things

but if they all go one way,
that's the way the wind goes.[v]

Later in his visit, Stafford told a story about "Note." He traveled extensively all over the world. Once, in Pakistan, he opened his bag for a customs official.

"Books," the man observed.

"I am a poet," said Stafford.

"And these are your books?" The official pulled *Allegiances* from a suitcase, and turned to "Note." He read the poem to Stafford, then closed the book. "I like it," he said. "Very nice. You may go."

Stafford liked that story because it confirmed his belief in the vibrant, living connection provided by language. Words, after all, are the little things of "Note." When they all go one way, they reveal the big thing—wind, place, poem, human connection.

I. STAFFORD AND THE PLACE OF LANGUAGE

"I can say without any problem that the language is what I live in when I write. –William Stafford[vi]

Stafford wrote a great deal about his writing method, especially in the two books of prose/poetry/interviews published by The University of Michigan Press in their Poets on Poetry series. *Writing the Australian Crawl* and *You Must Revise Your Life* are full of apt metaphors. For example, Stafford is starting a car on ice, developing a "traction on ice between writer and reader," making the reader enter a poem because "the moves . . . come from inside the poem, the coercion to be part of the life right there."[vii]

Or Stafford is dreaming, and making fun of those who treat dreaming/poetry as a business: "You extract from successful dreams the elements that work. Then you carefully fashion dreams of your own. This way, you can be sure to have admirable dreams, ones that will appeal to the educated public."[viii]

Or Stafford is swimming:

> Just as the swimmer does not have a succession of handholds hidden in the water, but instead simply sweeps that yielding medium and finds it hurrying him along, so the writer passes his attention through what is at hand, and is propelled by a medium too thin and all-pervasive for the perceptions of nonbelievers who try to stay on the bank and fathom his accomplishment[ix]

Or Stafford is rehearsing: "Maybe it is all rehearsal, even when practice/ ends and performance pretends to happen . . . Maybe your stumbling/ saves you, ..."[x]

Or Stafford is revising your life:

> We can all learn technique and then improvise pieces of writing again and again, but without a certain security of character we cannot sustain the vision, the trajectory of significant creation: we can learn and know and still not understand. Perceiving the need for that security of character is not enough—you have to possess it, and it is a gift, or something like a gift.[xi]

Or Stafford is climbing a cliff in the dark with scratched numb hands, muscles cracking. But he makes it to the top, to the finished poem and shouts: "Made it again! Made it again!"[xii]

These metaphors come out of Stafford's relationship to language, the paying attention to something bigger, becoming aware of what is big by paying attention to its "little things" and nudging forward based on his listening.

Nothing shows his relationship to language more than the manner of his own writing. He woke early each morning to write, because, as he says in "Freedom," "... most places,/ you can usually be free some of the time/ if you wake up before other people."[xiii] He sat in the dark, reclining on his couch, filling journal after journal. He was not writing poetry, he was writing. He was not crafting poems, he was listening. And what he listened to best was the language itself. Other writers have witnessed to the same thing. Joyce Thompson wrote what I as a writer believe. I think Stafford might agree with much of it:

> The language is often smarter than I am, than the writer is. I often feel like an idiot savant when I'm writing. It's a very intuitive process. There is a certain abrogation of ego, and it happens through the agent of language. It's difficult to explain that and I'm not sure it's the same for all writers. I know some people feel that composition is a real act of arrogance, and assertion of the ego, but I find that when the writing is going its best, it's a real absorption of the ego in the task, a laying aside of it. It's a pretty direct exchange between the language and whatever envisioned reality there is. I think that's one reason that I like doing it so much. I don't get in my own way nearly as much when I write as I do in some of the other things I do in life. There's something beyond individual self and I think, to an extent, I write to experience that.[xiv]

Language is the big sea for human beings. We swim in it, as Stafford said. We trust it, and it holds us up, sustains us. It is so much bigger than we are, and it is eternal—having a long life before us, and a long life after us. We do not master it, anymore than we master the water when we swim. But we do get to know it well, to use its strength, to hone our own efforts into an efficiency that makes us powerful because it is powerful. Sometimes, it is even more powerful than we are. I once asked Stafford if he'd ever written anything he didn't believe, if sometimes the poem dictated he move in a direction that wasn't quite right for him as a conscious person, but was right for the requirements of the poem. He didn't just answer yes, he answered, "Of course." As he wrote in "Some Arguments Against Good Diction,"

For people, the truth does not exist. But language offers a continuous encounter with our own laminated, enriched experiences; and sometimes those encounters lead to further satisfactions derived from the cumulative influences in language as it spins out.[xv]

The requirement of the poem—to be influenced by language—brings one to truth. Writing what the poem requires is different from manipulating language away from fact or truth. As a writer, Stafford was aware of that sad manipulation. In fact, he had a suspicion of idle conversation. He once said that in a dialogue he liked to leave with the feeling that "I listened better than he did."

I once had responsibility for Stafford when he visited the University of Kansas. I picked him up, took him to a party, and returned him to where he was staying. I followed him around at the party, a slightly fawning neophyte before the "great" man. Two-thirds of the way through the evening, I realized my hero had just told the same story for the third time. I was aghast. He was supposed to be the great listener, the swimmer, the one finding the next curve, the one most sensitive to nuance, to what might be unique in each question, each possible conversation. Most of all, this original man should have been original. This was my first experience separating the man from the poet, the party-goer-out-of-obligation from the self-disciplined-listener to the earth. I was later reassured by one of Stafford's poems:

At the Chairman's Housewarming

Talk like a jellyfish can ruin a party.
It did: I smiled whatever they said,
. . .
And my talk too—it poured on the table
and coiled and died in the sugar bowl,
twitching a last thin participle
to flutter the candle over its soul.
. . .
Oh go home, you terrible fish;
let sea be sea and rock be rock.
Go back wishy-washy to your sheltered bay,
but let me live definite, shock by shock.[xvi]

How wonderful, at the reading the next night, when Stafford's poetry lived definite, shock by shock, when the jellyfish of talk was replaced by the richness of language.

Stafford liked the experience of language so much he gave language and voice to most everything around him. His poems go beyond personification, that mere literary term, in the same way belief goes beyond technical explanation. When Native Americans, for example, pay attention to animals, to grass, to wind and leaf, we don't call it personification, we call it religion. I don't know what to call this same attention in Stafford's work, but it lives in lines like:

> air contains all. After
> we fall it waits. At the last
> it is frantic with its hands
> but cannot find us.
> Was it a friend? Now,
> too late, we think it was.
> That's why we became grass.[xvii]

For Stafford, everything, big and little—like straw, feathers and dust—has importance, has a name. Even the little seed that meets water in "B.C." speaks its stature: "Sequoia is my name."[xviii]

From little things, big things always grew. Over and over Stafford witnessed to his willingness for what came. "To get started I will accept anything that occurs to me."[xix] Or, "... most of what I write, like most of what I say in casual conversation, will not amount to much."[xx] And "Any little impulse is accepted, and enhanced."[xxi]

Stafford accepted and enhanced so much of his journal writing into poems, and he published so prolifically, that some critics chastised him for not being more selective. But he was prolific not because he was a poor critic of his own work, nor because he needed publication, nor because he was popular. He simply worked hard, shared enthusiastically, and believed more strongly in the process of writing than in the product of writing. His wise voice, his eager sharing, and the dailiness of his writing were always with him when he gave readings from his work.

At any William Stafford reading, everyone felt centered—in place, in language, in sensibility. He shared his work with humble enthusiasm, often giving a little tilt of his head at the end of a poem, as if to say, "What do you think of that?" He punctuated poems with talk, commentary, notes on composition, and then, halfway into a sentence, his audience would realize he wasn't talking anymore, he was reading the next poem. This gave witness to his definition of poetry: the ear of the reader shifts into attention. I never attended a Stafford reading when he didn't read from something he'd written that very morning, in the dark, reclining in a motel room. He engaged the world through language, constantly, and had amassed thousands of poems, his "notes," by the time of his death in August of 1993.

His last poem, titled "Are you Mr. William Stafford?" written August 28 of that year, the day he died, shows how true he was to language and to himself until the end. Some lines: "You can't tell when strange things with meaning/ will happen. I'm [still] here writing it down/ just the way it was."[xxii]

II. THE LANGUAGE OF PLACE

William Stafford sparked my interest in Kansas Literature when I first heard him read at the University of Kansas in the early '70s. His voice, his profound simplicity, his respect for our landscape, his desire to live by common things, his uncommon perspective on the world—he made these things Kansas.

Perhaps only someone born and raised in Central Kansas would say, "Mine was a Midwest Home—you can keep your world."[xxiii] Or, in giving voice to the subjects of Grant Woods' American Gothic: "If we see better through tiny/ grim glasses, we like to wear/ tiny, grim glasses."[xxiv] His wisdom, profound and simple, came in lines like: "Our Senator talked like war, and Aunt Mabel/ said, "He's a brilliant man,/ but we didn't elect him that much."[xxv] Or in "A Letter," when he writes the Governor about a little town that neither demands nor is afraid. He suggests, "You could think of that place annually/ on this date, for reassurance—a place where we have done no wrong."[xxvi] Stafford's wise pacifism—which has, I think, a corollary in his writing process, and is contained in so many poems—makes no demands, but asserts itself quietly in poems like "At the Un-National Monument Along the Canadian Border":

> This is the field where the battle did not happen,
> where the unknown soldier did not die....
> No people killed—or were killed—on this ground
> hallowed by neglect and an air so tame
> that people celebrate it by forgetting its name[xxvii]

Our landscape dwelled within him: "... somewhere inside, the clods are/ vaulted mansions, lines through the barn sing/ for the saints forever, the shed and windmill/ rear so glorious the sun shudders like a gong."[xxxviii] Or, "My self will be the plain,/ wise as winter is gray,/ pure as cold posts go/ pacing toward what I know."[xxix] Landscape and language and Stafford are all inseparable, here.

His lifelong celebration of little things, common things, real things, comes from a deep respect for the place he grew up. His poem "Allegiances" begins: "It is time for all the heroes to go home,/ if they have any, time for all of us common ones/ to locate ourselves by the real things/ we live by."[xxx] Every poem seemed to turn on seeing the depth in what was near: "In the yard I pray birds,/ wind, unscheduled grass,/ that they please help to make/ everything go deep again."[xxxi] and "World, I am your slow guest,/ one of the common things/ that move in the sun and have/ close, reliable friends/ in the earth, in the air, in the rock."[xxxii]

And his unique way of looking at the world is spoken like a Kansan. His poem, "Being an American," starts: "Some network has bought history,/ all the rights for wars and games." And ends: "Maybe even yet we could buy a little bit of today and see how it is."[xxxiii] His outsider critiques of contemporary life—as in "Have You Heard This One?"—would make any Kansan smile:

A woman forged her face.
(It was one she found in a magazine.)
Using it, she got a job on an airline.
One day a passenger said, "Haven't I seen
you everyplace before?" (He had been reading
Ring Lardner.) They got married
that very night in a motel.

This is a true story.
It happened in New York
and Los Angeles
and Chicago
and [...xxxiv]

Also very Kansan is Stafford's desire—in the collections of poetry, and in his readings—To put his reader/audience at ease. Note how many poems he wrote that introduce or say farewell, that create a climate of companionship. His first book, *West of Your City,* begins with the poem "Midwest," which invites the reader to "Come west and see; touch these leaves."[xxxv] The final poem of that collection, "Postscript," asks: "You reading this page, this trial—/ shall we portion out the fault?"[xxxvi] Other poems of greeting and departure include lines like, "Reader, we are in such a story:/ all of this is trying to arrange a kind of a prayer for you."[xxxvii] In these kinds of poems, Stafford is not only creating companionship, he is writing with the language of conversation, and he is engaging the reader into his way of writing and thinking about poetry. These poems are courteous beginnings, fond farewells: they speak to Stafford's theories of poetry and to his Kansas upbringing.

Stafford wants an engaged, rather than a pressured, reader. He also strived for engaged, not pressured, poems. Stafford rarely pushes a poem in any one particular place: no flashy beginnings, no endings with hammering closures. As my colleague Jim Hoogenakker said, "No rhyming couplets at the ends of sonnets in Stafford."[xxxviii] In fact, Stafford frequently wrote lines like "What the river says, that's what I say," even though it's not a statement, it's a metaphor. He never tells us what the river says. In "Put These in Your Pipe" he writes, "I think of something to end with,/ but I'm not going to write it down."[xxxix] In "Notice What This Poem Is Not Doing" he uses that line as a refrain, then ends with the line "Notice what this poem has not done."[xl] Stafford is always digging rather than telling.

Some of his work is almost underdone, as in poems like "Things I Learned Last Week," where he sets these two stanzas against each other:

Yeats, Pound, and Eliot saw art as
growing from other art. They studied that.

If I ever die, I'd like it to be
in the evening. That way, I'll have
all the dark to go with me, and no one
will see how I begin to hobble along.[xli]

This quality of the underdone, understated, is also part of Stafford's unwillingness to assert beyond the self. As such, there is a sort of Kansas definite indefiniteness that is akin to privacy. When he ends "The Farm on the Great Plains" with the line "pacing toward what I know"[xlii] the reader realizes that something is being withheld. What is

186

he pacing toward? Why won't he say? He will say: he'll say what the river says. What the stone posts know. And no more.

Stafford's use of language is like the landscape of Kansas, spare but incredibly full of subtle beauty and remnants of the historical past. Part of that past is pioneering. In "One Home" he writes, "To anyone who looked at us we said, `My friend';/ liking the cut of a thought, we could say `Hello.'"[xliii] This is still the code in Western Kansas, where a wave is returned, where anyone near is better than nobody. "American Gothic" ends, "Poverty plus confidence equals/ pioneers. We never doubted."[xliv] Stafford's work has that same pluck: humble materials plus confidence equals poetic innovation.

The humble materials are simple words, simply used. But, as Stafford writes in "How These Words Happened," "... I found these words and put them/ together by their appetites and respect for/ each other. In stillness, they jostled. They traded/ meanings while pretending to have only one."[xlv] Being satisfied with humble materials is part of what the earth says in Kansas. Stafford's "In Response to a Question" has a litany: The earth says "have a place, be what that place/ requires;" "have a ranch/ that's minimum: one tree, one well," "wear the kind/ of color that your life is (gray shirt for me)"; and yet for all the simplicity, the poem asserts the riches and loss of this flat place, with its "flat evening," its "sparrow on the lawn," its wind, its ritual for the wavering," its "sermon of the hills," its "highway guided by the way the world is tilted." And the end comes with lack of assertion: "Listening, I think that's what the earth says."[xlvi] The "I think" of that last line mirrors what I tend to think of as the Kansas affection for qualifiers, at least I kind of think it does, pretty much.

Remember, too, that Stafford doesn't want the perfect poem. He cultivated imperfection by giving himself over to language, rather than trying to control it. As he says at the beginning of "At the Fair": "Even the flaws were good—"[xlvii] Stafford had a healthy mistrust of technique:

> When I'm writing, I'm not at all trying to fit in any forms, . . .
> That doesn't seem to me the crucial or essential thing, . . . [My] composition . . . is not a technique, it's a kind of stance to take toward experience, or an attitude to take toward immediate feelings and thoughts while you're writing. That seems important to me, but technique is something I believe I would like to avoid.[xlviii]

187

Tradition was suspect:

> Even those of us who are critics, teachers, scholars, have always
> trafficked in something much more precious than our rules could
> identify; and now with the help of kindergartners, protesters,
> joshing conversationalists, and disporting scholars, we have
> glimpsed how language belongs to all of us, and poetry does too.
> . . . Poetry today grows from a tradition that is wider than just the
> sequence of poems we inherit. The language all speakers use is
> the tradition.[xlix]

Even meaning was something to avoid. Stafford didn't want
poems that could be explained by what he called "the explainers," but
poems defined by the attention of the reader. The first stanza of "The
Trouble With Reading" speaks to the difference between paying
attention and dissecting for meaning:

> When a goat likes a book, the whole book is gone,
> and the meaning has to go find an author again.
> But when we read, it's just print—deciphering,
> like frost on a window: we learn the meaning
> but lose what the frost is, and all that world
> pressed so desperately behind.[l]

Stafford's definition of poetry is reader-based. In the essay "Making a
Poem/Starting a Car on Ice," he calls a poem "anything said in such a
way or put on the page in such a way as to invite from the hearer or
reader a certain kind of attention."[li] In "You and Art," Stafford wrote,

> Your exact errors make a music
> that nobody hears.
> Your straying feet find the great dance,
> walking alone.
> And you live on a world where stumbling
> always leads home.[lii]

After his oldest son, Bret, committed suicide in November of
1988, I wrote a letter to Stafford expressing my dismay, and my best
wishes to him. He wrote back, "True, we did suffer a grievous blow;
it was a jagged event. But the little things, and letters like yours, have
brought us around. I see things differently, hear music better, and

value friends even more than before."[liii] As in art, the stumbling, the straying, the errors, all converge into meaning. Not the big meaning of philosophy, but the small meanings of a life lived.[liv]

I consider Stafford's respect for the flawed, for error, as well as his disrespect for technique and tradition to be part of his nature as a Kansan. We Kansans joke that our lives are "pretty good," our state "not bad," our towns "fair to middling." Of course, we know how profound our experience is, how much we are a part of a natural world that signals to us each day. We live under a huge sky, and, as a people with roots in agriculture, we learn to accept what is, and take what comes. Survival is not a philosophy, it's our activity, and it teaches us a kind of humility. That's the landscape we live in. Look at one of my favorite Stafford poems:

Passing Remark

In scenery I like flat country.
In life, I don't like much to happen.

In personalities I like mild colorless people.
And in colors I prefer gray and brown.

My wife, a vivid girl from the mountains,
says, "Then why did you choose me?"

Mildly I lower my brown eyes—
there are so many things admirable people do not understand.[lv]

A lot of people might not understand Stafford's affection for Kansas—anyone's affection for Kansas, for that matter. I trace mine to my parents' love of the place they made home and family. In 1997, I met Stafford's second son Kim for lunch in Oregon. We had much in common—both second born sons of good fathers recently lost, the same number of siblings, the recent birth of a child. I shared a piece of writing my psychiatrist father had done. In his article, he described the importance, in the therapeutic process, of what he called the "lost good object." He defined that as a person, place, or relationship that, if remembered and explored, would affirm the best in life, would create positive movement, would lead to healing and sanity. I sent Kim the article. Later, we spoke on the phone: "Kansas was my father's lost good object," Kim said.[lvi] Others might call Kansas

Stafford's inspiration, or touchstone, or grounding. But, in part because of William Stafford, Kansas has become a richer, more celebrated place.[lvii]

III. STAFFORD AS PLACE

> Without a shield of hills, a barricade
> of elms, one resorts to magic, hiding
> the joker well behind the gesturing hand.
> —Richard Hugo, "In Stafford Country"

For Kansas poetry, after Stafford—his first book was *West of Your City*, 1960—William Stafford became "the way it is." He was and still is the profound influence. Like the landscape itself, Stafford inspired writers. Because, in some ways, he has become Kansas, his life and work are a kind of landscape.

Stafford traveled a great deal, and met many writers. His letters were full of what he variously called, "the academic swirl," the "circuit," or "zigzag jaunt," the "swirls of sociability," the "good encounters" and "engagements."[lviii]

Almost every writer I've met has a Stafford story. Ohio Poet Grace Butcher visited Washburn a couple of times. I was pumping her for exercises to use with young writers in the classroom. She suggested one she'd done recently: take an experience from the past in which you behaved badly, and rewrite yourself as a decent person, doing the right thing. "William Stafford did that one with us once," she said. "It's in A Glass Face in the Rain." I looked up "One Time," a poem about a blind girl Stafford finds on the schoolground in the darkening evening. He hears things as she hears them, a "great sprinkler arm of water" finding the pavement, "pigeons telling each other their dreams." He writes that he said,

> ... "Tina, it's me—
> Hilary says I should tell you it's dark,
> and, oh, Tina, it is. Together now—"
>
> And I reached, our hands touched,
> and we found our way home.[lix]

Both Grace Butcher and I wondered what Bill Stafford was re-writing—what slight was he making up for in his encounter with that

190

blind girl? Or was he re-writing an imagined moment that lived only in the language?

Many writers tip their hats to Stafford in direct and indirect ways. Denise Low, Lawrence poet who teaches at Haskell Indian Nations University, and who edited The Kansas Poems of William Stafford wrote a poem for him, "Kansas Grasslands, for William Stafford." The last stanza:

> This imperfect circle is Stafford's horizon,
> a curved line to keep stars from spilling,
> a line through air, a thatched edge—
> the path he traveled skyward and back.[lx]

Richard Hugo tried to capture the landscape of Kansas' great poet with "In Stafford Country":

> ... With homes exposed
> no wonder people love. Farms absorb
> the quiet of the snow, and birds
> are black and nameless miles away.
> ...
> Where land is flat, words are far apart.
> Each word is seen, coming from far off,
> a calm storm, almost familiar, across
> the plain.[lxi]

Flint Hills-bred Steven Hind, who teaches at Hutchinson Community College, tried for years after Stafford's death to pay tribute to Stafford—his language and spirit. He once wrote to me in an e-mail: "I woke up with a Stafford line in my head: `What the river says, that is what I say' (`Ask Me'). And I scribbled out my own little confirmation of . . . what water does when it lands on earth."[lxii]

Decision

> When our river had a change
> of heart and gouged south,
> saying so long to its last
> northerly horseshoe, trees
> sent descendants, and weeds
> webbed the dark earth between

saplings under elders stirring
in the high breezes. And that
growth-choked channel where
our river wasn't wore a new
slogan: long live volunteers.[lxiii]

And for the 1996 Stafford conference at Kansas State University Hind
read one he really thought he got right:

A Chosen Way
    "... judge me: I came away." from "Prairie Town"

    This Bill of art and right paused at
    a fence one day and saw prairie
    dogs perched at their doors.

    "Citizens," he heard the day saying
    in its own strange way, "I grant
    you rights to your town."

    Then he turned back for the town
    where he had slept the stretching
    nights and cored the light in his way.

    He followed to the river south of town
    and felt the current in his fingers,
    felt the trustworthy flow, baptizing
    that hand chosen for life.[lxiv]

But my favorite of Hind's Stafford poems is one in which he tries to
capture the feel of Stafford's "Being an American":

Stafford Ball Back Home

We never report our scores.
No one in our league does.
Our uniforms are camouflage
jerseys and shorts. We play
in the old cow lot and change
the rules, once we know them.
It's exciting, in a curious way.

The lazy give up and go pro,
if they're big enough. Sometimes,
we all get a trophy: Least Valuable
Player. I won again last week.[lxv]

When we work with Stafford, we all win—readers, poets, writers, scholars, Kansans.

Stafford visited Washburn shortly after having been commissioned to write a poem for a Portland restaurant. He was taken by the request, and came up with "Ode to Garlic," later published in An Oregon Message. He sent me a broadside of the poem, inscribed, and it hangs on my dining room wall. I was inspired to write a garlic poem, as well, though as part of an exercise for my creative writing class. I admired Stafford's admiration of garlic's intensity:
... you learn
from garlic—how to taste the world:
the anticipation, the pleasure,
the living with it, always there,
in your every breath.

Stafford, like nature itself, was always willing to share. He was so enthusiastic in person and in letters that he buoyed those of us who aspired to be writers. The final lines of "Ode to Garlic" seem to be about more than garlic. They speak to Stafford and his poetry itself: "You walk out generously, giving it back/ in a graceful wave, what you've been given./ Like a child again, you breathe on the world, and it shines."[lxvi] No poet I know could make the world shine like Stafford could.

As we leave our gathering, we must leave breathing Stafford's words. Two days before his death, he wrote "You Reading This, Be Ready." The final two lines make a fit end for us, as well: "What can anyone give you greater than now,/ starting here, right in this room, when you turn around?"[lxvii]

"I would also like to mention aluminum."[lxviii]

i. William Stafford, *The Way It Is: New & Selected Poems* (Saint Paul, Minnesota: Graywolf Press, 1998), p. 126. Future citations to this book will be abbreviated, *TWII*, followed by the page number.

ii. William Stafford, *Kansas Poems of William Stafford*, edited and with an introduction by Denise Low (Topeka, Kansas: Woodley Press, 1990) p. vi. Future citations to this book will be abbreviated *KP*, followed by the page number of the poem.

iii. William Stafford, *Writing the Australian Crawl, Views on the Writer's Vocation* (Ann Arbor, Michigan: The University of Michigan Press, 1978), p. 65. Future references to this book will be abbreviated *WAC*.

viii. William Stafford, *You Must Revise Your Life* (Ann Arbor, Michigan: The University of Michigan Press, 1986), p. 52. Future references to this book will be abbreviated *YMRYL*.

ix. *WAC*, pp. 25-26.

x. *YMRYL*, from "Practice," p. 34.

xi. Ibid, from "An Invitation to the Reader," p. ix.

xii. Ibid., from "After Arguing against the Contention That Art Must Come from Discontent," p. 28.

xiii. *TWII*, p. 142.

xiv. From an interview with Joyce Thompson, in "Writer's Ask," Issue No. 10, 2001, Glimmer Train Press, Inc., np.

xv. *WAC*, p. 60.

xvi. *TWII*, p. 113.

xvii. William Stafford, *Stories That Could Be True, New and Collected Poems* (New York: Harper & Row, 1977), p. 179. Future references to this book will be abbreviated *STCBT*, followed by the page number of the poem.

xviii. Ibid., p. 87.

xix. *WAC*, p. 17.

xx. Ibid., p. 19.

xxi. Ibid., p. 49.

xxii. *TWII*, p. 46.

xxiii. *KP*, p. 7.

xxiv. Ibid., p. 23.

xxv. *TWII*, p. 111.

xxvi. *STCBT*, p. 171.

xxvii. Ibid., p. 17. See also, *KP*, "How My Mother Carried on Her Argument With the World," pp. 31-32.

xxviii. *TWII*, p. 129.

xxix. Ibid., p. 64.

xxx. Ibid., p. 128.

[xxxi]. William Stafford, *Allegiances* (New York: Harper & Row, 1970), p. 58. Future references to this book will be abbreviated *A*, followed by the page number of the poem.

[xxxii]. Ibid., p. 12.

[xxxiii]. *TWII*, p. 217.

[xxxiv]. *STCBT*, p. 245.

[xxxv]. Ibid., p. 29.

[xxxvi]. Ibid., p. 57.

[xxxvii]. Ibid., p. 147.

[xxxviii]. The English Department at Washburn University teaches Stafford's work in the Freshman Honors English course, and my colleagues Jim Hoogenakker and Robert Stein have studied Stafford's work with their students for years now. I thank them and my poet colleague Amy Fleury for their attentive suggestions as I put together these remarks.

[xxxix]. *TWII*, p. 20.

[xl]. Ibid., p. 178.

[xli]. Ibid., p. 195.

[xlii]. Ibid., p. 64.

[xliii]. Ibid., p. 61.

[xliv]. *KP*, p. 23.

[xlv]. *TWII*, p. 251.

[xlvi]. Ibid., p. 86.

[xlvii]. *STCBT*, p. 130.

[xlviii]. *WAC*, p. 98.

[xlix]. Ibid., p. 77 and p. 79.

[l]. *TWII*, p. 237.

[li]. *WAC*, p. 61.

[lii]. *TWII*, p. 7.

[liii]. Personal correspondence between William Stafford and the author, 28 Feb 89.

[liv]. Stafford wrote a poem after his son's suicide. See "A Memorial: Son Bret," *TWII*, p. 16.

[lv]. *TWII*, p. 116.

[lvi]. Phone conversations from February 1998 and March 2001, Kim Stafford.

[lvii]. For my father's article see, Stuart Carson Averill, MD, "Recovery of the lost good object," *Bulletin of the Menninger Clinic*, Vol. 61, No. 3 (Summer 1997), pp. 288-296.

[lviii]. Personal correspondence, Stafford to Averill, 22 Nov 74, 23 February 1976, 26 April 76, 9 November 76 and 11 Jan 78.

[lix]. William Stafford, *A Glass Face in the Rain* (New York: Harper & Row, 1982), p. 106.

[lx]. Denise Low, *New and Selected Poems, 1980-1999* (Lawrence, Kansas: Penthe Press, 1999), p. 8.

[lxi]. Richard Hugo, *Making Certain It Goes On, The Collected Poems of Richard Hugo* (New York: W.W. Norton, 1984), pp. 91-92.

[lxii]. E-mail to author, 25 Jan 1995.

[lxiii]. Steven Hind, *In A Place With No Map* (Topeka, Kansas: Center for Kansas Studies/Woodley Press, 1997), p. 6.

[lxiv]. In a letter to the author, March 15, 2001.

[lxv]. E-mail to author, 16 Feb 1996.

[lxvi]. *TWII,* p. 224.

[lxvii]. Ibid., p. 45.

[lxviii]. *WAC,* p. 140.

AFTERWARD 2010

By Denise Low

I.

What courage it took in 1960, the year William Stafford published *West of Your City*, to extol the "Midwest," "Far West," and "Outside"—the book's three regional sections. That year W.D. Snodgrass won the Pulitzer Prize in poetry for *Heart's Needle*, a volume of patterned poems set firmly in the British tradition. Snodgrass's title poem begins with an epigram from The Middle-Irish Romance *The Madness of Suibhne*. Stafford's hard scrabble verse was outside this aesthetic. Most courageous in *West of Your City* is the section of agricultural poems, which were unlikely topics for highbrow poetry.

Wes Jackson of The Land Institute has written how the trajectory of the American imagination goes from rural to urban: Farming represents the nostalgic past; cities are the future (93). In 1900, 90% of America was rural. By 1960, less than 10% of the population lived in rural areas. Even the older Turner Hypothesis shows the (exciting) frontier moving from East to West (another paradigm for past to future), through the prairies to Oregon or California. Either way, the heartland is passé, wasteland with wheel ruts, the cultural version of the Great American Desert.

Stafford embraced this stark setting. He mythologized it, and even though he spent the last half of his life in Oregon, the Great Plains informed his writing. He created his own vocabulary, filled with numerous metaphors for sky, sight, grass, horizon, river, time, stars, hope, wind, and conviction. As a young poet, I learned his language and saw an American-sited present. His writings were not the first about the central Pains—Kenneth Wiggins Porter and others preceded Stafford's publishing history. But he was the best.

II.

William Stafford succeeded nationally because his skilled poems, so place-centered, transcended place. He leapt before Robert Bly explained "leaping" poetry as "a jump from an object soaked in unconscious substance to an object or idea soaked in conscious psychic substance." This is the essence of Stafford's verse, its

movement from outer to inner sightedness, and back out again, but
with a twist. He uses extreme personifications, with the same method
as John Donne's metaphors. According to Donne, two lovers are
hands of a compass. According to Stafford, time can wave backwards.
Stafford re-creates the world into a dimension with multiple
timelines. The poem "At the Breaks Near the River," in this volume,
follows Stafford's individualized formula of leaps among places,
times, and imagined realities:

> Autumn some year will discover again
> that gesture of the flattened grass, wild
> on the Cimarron hills when a storm
> out of northern New Mexico raided
> Cheyenne country to hunt for rusty armor
> left by Coronado, and my father sifting his
> fingers in that loose ground of the Indian
> campsite said, "Oh, Bill, to know
> everything! Look—the whole world is alive,
> waving together toward history!"

Cimarron River hills are a definite place in southwest Kansas, in the
path of New Mexico winds, yet the entire poem transposes to an
imagined, conditional mood—something that *could* happen— by use
of the indefinite "some year." Time moves from seasonal cycles to
historic ones to the poem's eternal present—and again to a past-
perfect (that which started in the past and ended in the past) *future*:
"the whole world" of Cheyenne dominance and Coronado's
excursions remains "alive" and "waving" in this future. The trick of
the poem is the last line, where instead of looking backwards at
history, the narrator and the father see history as a future memory of
the present. This is an invented verb tense. Perspectives pivot like this
within all of Stafford's language scrims.

Yet another Staffordean trick is the unlikely personification of the
intangible "Autumn," which will "discover again . . . ." The poem
reinforces the father's assertion that "the whole world is alive." Such
animism not only concerns the natural world, but also the fluid
elements of the entire cosmos.

The moral of this short verse is: "Look." These brief lines are an
example of the kind of "looking" that Stafford's "father" urges.

III.

Stafford's family typifies the Kansas heritage. Under his mild, agreeable manner rested a will of iron ore. Convictions appear in many Kansans, whether their beliefs are creationism or pacifism. As the Pilgrims were outcasts from England for their religion, and Mennonites in Central Kansas were Pacifists who fled German conscription, many folks in the Great Plains were outsiders who did not fit orthodoxies. They sacrificed for their religious or political views. My own family has Quakers who were cast out of the church for nonconformity and Abolitionists who left the South. Stafford's status as a conscientious objector during World War II, shared by neighboring Mennonites, was not an easy position. He told me it led to his eventual relocation outside the state, after the war, when feelings were high against this stance.

I encountered this steely side of Stafford one evening during conversation about a Kansas anthology I had just edited. The organizing principle was residency in the state, and he objected strongly that I had omitted him and included William S. Burroughs, a Lawrence resident. He was polite, but I was made to understand his feelings fully. He clearly did not approve of Burroughs.

Stafford also communicated with me about his American Indian heritage—not uncommon for Kansans of this region. Stafford wrote me April 17, 1990, "Yes, my father told me we do have Indian ancestry (one of my several claims for inclusion in anthologies!)" and again June 8, 1990, "About our Indianness, yes, my father used to remind me that we had some Indian background, and he always made me feel near to it." In 1994 his son Kim told me the Native relatives originated in Ohio, where many Eastern tribes found refuge, including my own Bear and Root families. Siouan, Algonquin, and some Iroquoian bands were exiled west, incrementally, and in the early to mid-19th century, many resided in Ohio.

In Stafford's autobiographical verse, his part-Native father mediates between the natural and social environments. This contemporary father is situated within the world rather than outside it, as in "At the Breaks Near the River." Rather than observing a separate otherness about the Cheyenne campsite, the father touches it and explains the continuum. The "Indian" does not remain in a reified past. The poem celebrates this reality, among the strands of past and future.

Like many people of some Native heritage, Stafford does not presume an intact tradition—in his 1984 interview with Steven Hind he notes how "fractioned" Americans are. Nonetheless he chooses to subvert European concepts like wilderness, mind-body duality, and the Ptolemaic concept, where sun and planets orbit around Earth, the human center. Each of Stafford's poems makes the point that people are among, not over, the many species. The world is alive, in ways we cannot easily understand, but these poems, set on this continent, are a guide.

IV.

In his poetry William Stafford preserves a small town proscenium around collective historic memories. The iconic Midwestern play *Our Town* seldom appears on today's required reading lists, yet Stafford depends on a similar small town setting to represent a larger idea of moral responsibilities. "Thinking for Berky" (reprinted in this volume) is one of his best known poems, about an outcast teenage girl whose poverty makes her vulnerable to sexual exploitation and danger. The narrator concludes:

> There are things not solved in our town though tomorrow came:
> There are things time passing can never make come true.
> We live in an occupied country, misunderstood;
> justice will take us millions of intricate moves.

"Our town" here is the Greek chorus, it is Thornton Wilder's 1938 play, and it is the small Kansas town where every person is familiar and judged. It provides a minimalist setting where moral issues have stark outlines.

In "Serving with Gideon" Stafford examines racial bias, beginning with the first stanza:

> Now I remember: in our town the druggist
> prescribed Coca-Cola mostly, in tapered
> glasses to us, and to the elevator
> man in a paper cup, so he could
> drink it elsewhere because he was black. (*The Way It Is* 213)

In the poem, he contrasts the elevator attendant to the town fathers, with their "gambling / in the back room, and no women, but girls, / old boys who ran the town." and he chooses to stand against petty nepotism, sexism and prejudice when, "I walked with my cup toward the elevator man." Twice in the poem he notes he could have been in that back room also, but he made a moral choice.

Racial prejudice was not a hypothetical situation. In the 1930s, Stafford remembers discrimination at the University of Kansas:

Some of us would go into the café at the Union and have a sit-in, to break down the policy against serving blacks—"Negroes," in those days.... Whites and blacks could not sit together and be served. So we would sit apart, be served, then take our food and sit down together. (*You Must Revise Your Life* 10)

Stafford was a revolutionary, decades before the Civil Rights movement. In Kansas, a border state, his strong convictions played against a backdrop of narrow, stratified social relationships. Yet they could be expressed openly. Like Langston Hughes's efforts in Lawrence a few decades before, Stafford's activism must have had some effect, if only to keep a door open.

I have wondered if Stafford's own background of poverty and mixed heritages helped strengthen his stance. His own father traveled from town to town trying to find employment. Stafford told me of his own fiscal problems during the Depression as a college student. He and a friend cultivated a truck farm by the Kansas River to support themselves. The mule died, and Stafford himself pulled the plow. Stafford understood, like former hobo Loren Eiseley, the desperation of hunger.

He also understood small town life as both nurturing and punishing. The poem "One Home," in this volume, gives a bleak indictment of the social realm: "Plain black hats rode the thoughts that made our code." His poem "American Gothic," based on Grant Wood's 1930 painting, satirizes his heritage:

If we see better through tiny,
grim glasses, we like to wear
tiny, grim glasses.
Our parents willed us this

view. It's tundra? We love it. (*Kansas Poems*)

Both the black hat and the "tiny, grim glasses" are artificial and suggest limitation, stricture, and distortion. These contrast to the multiple dimensions of the grasslands, rivers, stars, wind—past the edge of towns and cultivated fields, as in "The Peters Family":

> At the end of their ragged field
> a new field began:
> miles told the sunset that Kansas
> would hardly ever end. . . . (*Kansas Poems*)

V.

Stafford was a humble man. He understood, as a prolific writer, that some of his writings were better than others. My first encounter with him was in 1977, when editor Mike Smetzer solicited poems for the *Cottonwood Review*. As a new associate editor, I was amazed to see a poet of his stature submit a group of poems that was uneven, and Smetzer rejected some. Nonetheless, all the correspondence from the poet was remarkably courteous. Some years later I would hear Stafford say in a reading, "Editors are our friends. They save us from publishing bad poems."

He understood writers' vulnerabilities, and this attitude was apparent when I corresponded with him about the first edition of *Kansas Poems of William Stafford*. In 1989 he wrote me, "I'm glad the Kansas poems project is rolling—how I hope my poems will provide you with a worthy text."—this from a man who had won the National Book Award. When the project was nearly completed, he wrote, "Your packet of material makes me feel great. I'd like to deserve such care and insight as you offer." I remember my own Kansas father worrying that I might grow up to be "swell-headed," apparently one of the worst fates, and here I saw Stafford keeping his head in proper proportion throughout his life, despite a national reputation.

Not that Stafford hid his light under a bushel. He responded immediately to any solicitation, often by return mail. When I asked to reprint Harper & Row poems for the anthology, he referred me to their permissions department to experience New York publishers for myself. I learned the economic reality, which was $5 a line—and that was the 1989 rate. I remember the clipped, fast voice of the permissions editor squeezed through the telephone as she delivered this news. I was standing in the attic semidarkness of Washburn University's Morgan Hall, offices of Woodley Press, which made the encounter seem even more unreal. I understood, then, why some of the poet's longer poems like "In Sublette's Barn" are seldom reprinted. I understood that not all business was conducted with a handshake.

I better appreciated how generous Stafford was. He donated his time and poems to the project without expectation of gain:

> You ask about terms I'd like, and I don't know what to say—total ignorance. Is there some guideline? ... I'm ready to bet on our book, take a chance. In other words, I'd rather share the risks with no money up front if that would help. Or copies of the book. I'm adjustable; I'm from Kansas. (26 June 1990)

When *Kansas Poems of William Stafford* was first published by Woodley Press, a very small enterprise, he offered promotional help throughout the country. He was an organized businessman when it came to getting his work into the world. He sent me one season's itinerary, and it was an entire singled-spaced page of events across the continent.

Stafford was also generous with praise, as he made these comments after receiving the finished book:

> And I am pleased and awed by your wide net for poems. What a search it must have been! I gloat over having these "home" poems together in one book. I guess all the time I have been spreading work around I have felt wistful about scattering my home feelings so widely. Now I can take a good look at the center of my life. (8 June 1990)

These kind words meant a lot to me at the time. Stafford was almost the same age as my father, and as this correspondence occurred, my own father was disabled by a stroke. I had burdens of assisting my mother with arrangements as well as grieving the virtual death of my father. He lived another ten years as an invalid, without speech or the ability to walk. Stafford's encouraging presence in my life helped ease the difficulties, as well as the encouragement of Bob Lawson, Woodley editor, Philip Miller, Stephen Meats, and other Woodley board members. Without these supports, I would have never finished the task.

Stafford's comments also give insight into his own ideas about Kansas as "home" and as "center of my life." His son Kim writes about this perspective about Kansas also:

> His Kansas patriotism saturated our childhoods. Any topic that arose in family conversation would—like water seeking the sea—arrive eventually at some comparison with Kansas. "In *Kansas*," my father would say with emphasis, and then the authority of perfection—good or bad—would be revealed: the best kind of evening, the most pungent smell, the most unusual gossip, the strangest character. My father's Kansas legends were behind all we did as a family, the places we went, the people we met. His private writings show how Kansas informed his experience. (*Early Morning* 28)

So it is fitting that this new edition of *Kansas Poems of William Stafford* continues the legends and the values of one of the best Kansans.

Bly, Robert. *Leaping Poetry: An Idea with Poems and Translations.* Boston: Beacon Press, 1975.

Jackson, Wes. *Altars of Unhewn Stone: Science and the Earth.* San Francisco: North Point Press, 1987. 93.

Snodgrass, William. *Heart's Needle.* 1959. Rpt. New York: Knopf Doubleday, 1983.

Stafford, Kim. *Early Morning: Remembering My Father.* St. Paul: Graywolf, 2002.

Stafford, William. *The Way It Is: New & Selected Poems.* Graywolf: St. Paul, 2002.

-----*You Must Revise Your Life.* Ann Arbor: University of Michigan, 1986.

-----*West of Your City.* Los Gatos: Talisman Press, 1960.

Letters are in the Leonard H. Axe Library at Pittsburg State University.

WILLIAM STAFFORD RESOURCES

The William Stafford Archive, directed by Paul Merchant. Diane McDevitt is the Archive Assistant. Vincent Wixon is the Archive Scholar-in-Residence. Kim Stafford is the Literary Executor of the Estate of William Stafford, of which the Archive forms the core.
http://williamstaffordarchives.org/

Kim Stafford's home page with William Stafford resources, including an index to poems published in his 60 books.
http://www.kim-stafford.com/

Lewis & Clark College materials. William Stafford and Kim Stafford taught at Lewis & Clark College in Oregon for many years.
http://legacy.lclark.edu/~krs/archive.html

William Stafford Archives Blog: A blog to announce ongoing developments at the William Stafford Archives and to receive reader commentaries. Annual announcements of William Stafford birthday readings are announced here.
http://williamstaffordarchives.blogspot.com/

To join the "Friends of William Stafford," contact Patricia Wixon, Friends of William Stafford, 126 Church St., Ashland, OR 97520.
http://www.wmstafford.org/

The William Edgar Stafford Collection of the Leonard H. Axe Library, Pittsburg State University, Pittsburg, Kansas
http://library.pittstate.edu/spcoll/ndxstafford.html

Calendar of William Stafford-Denise Low Correspondence, Leonard H. Axe Library, Pittsburg State University, Pittsburg, Kansas
http://library.pittstate.edu/spcoll/stafford-low.html

CONTRIBUTORS

Thomas Fox Averill is Writer-in-residence and Professor of English at Washburn University of Topeka. His story collections are *Passes at the Moon* (Woodley Press), *Seeing Mona Naked* (Watermark Press), and *Ordinary Genius* (University of Nebraska Press). He is the editor of *What Kansas Means to Me* (University Press of Kansas). Eagle Books (Wichita) brought out his *Oleader's Guide to Kansas*. His novels are *Secrets of the Tsil Cafe* (BlueHen/Putnam) and *The Slow Air of Ewan MacPherson* (BlueHen/Berkley). He helped to found, and was the first director of, Washburn's Center for Kansas Studies. He has recent publications in *New Letters*, *Cimarron Review*, *Chariton Review*, *North American Review* and *Doubletake*.

Kirsten Bosnak is a graduate student pursuing an MFA from the University of Kansas. Her thesis project is interviews with notable Kansas poets. She lives and gardens near the Kansas River in North Lawrence. She is communications director for the Native Medicinal Plant Research Program at the University of Kansas. She has previous publication in *Flint Hills Review* and the *New Mexico Review.*

Robert Day's novel *The Last Cattle Drive* was a Book-of-the-Month Club selection. He is the author of two novellas, as well as *Speaking French in Kansas* (short stories). Recent publications are *We Should Have Come By Water* (poems, Mammoth) and *The Committee to Save the World* (literary nonfiction, Western Books). Among his awards are: a National Endowment for the Arts Creative Writing Fellowship, Yaddo and McDowell Fellowships, a Maryland Arts Council Award, two Seaton Prizes, a Pen Faulkner/NEA prize, and Best American Short Stories, Pushcart citations, and the Edgar Wolfe Award. His teaching positions include The Iowa Writers Workshop; The University of Kansas; and the Graduate Faculty at Montaigne College, The University of Bordeaux. He is an Adjunct Professor of English Literature at Washington College.

Steven Hind is a native of the Flint Hills and a poet. His collections include *Familiar Ground, That Trick of Silence, In a Place With No Map,* and *The Loose Change of Wonder.* He graduated from the University of Kansas and Emporia State University with degrees in English. He taught many years at Hutchinson Community College.

Jonathan Holden, Kansas' first poet laureate (2005-2007), is a University Distinguished Professor of English and Poet-in-Residence at Kansas State University, Manhattan. Holden has won including, twice, a National

Endowment for the Arts Creative Writing Fellowship. In 1995, poet Yusef Komunyakaa chose Holden's poetry collection *The Sublime* for the Vassar Miller Prize. He has published twenty books of poetry, fiction, memoir, and literary criticism. In 1986, he received the Kansas State University Distinguished Faculty Award. Holden earned his bachelor's degree in 1963 in English from Oberlin College, his master's degree in 1970 in English with creative writing from San Francisco State College, and his doctorate in 1974 in English from the University of Colorado. He has been at Kansas State University since 1978.

Denise Low, Kansas Poet Laureate 2007-2009, has been writing, reviewing, editing and publishing literary and scholarly articles for 30 years. She is the author of ten collections of poetry and six books of essays, including a biography of Langston Hughes (co-authored with Thomas Pecore Weso). She has edited anthologies about Laguna Pueblo author Leslie Marmon Silko, environment, and local cultures. Her writing appears in *North American Review, Midwest Quarterly, Connecticut Review, Chariton Review,* and others. She has been a faculty member and administrator at Haskell Indian Nations University and visiting full professor at University of Kansas (2008) and University of Richmond (2005). She serves on the board of the Associated Writing Programs Association. She has awards from the National Endowment for the Humanities, Lannan Foundation, Poetry Society of America, Roberts Foundation, The Newberry Library, and others.

Caryn Mirriam-Goldberg is the 2009-2011 Poet Laureate of Kansas. She is founder of Transformative Language Arts at Goddard College, where she teaches in a low-residency program. Her books include four collections of poetry; a memoir on cancer, community and ecology, *The Sky Begins At Your Feet;* an award-winning writing guide, *Write Where You Are;* and an anthology on Transformative Language Arts. She received her Ph.D. and MA from the University of Kansas. She is the recipient of Kansas Arts Fellowship in Poetry, the Rocky Mountain National Park artist-in-residency, the City of Lawrence Phoenix Award, and other honors.

Al Ortolani, from Pittsburg, Kansas, is a career secondary education teacher who graduated from Pittsburg State University. He has taught English in the Baxter Springs, Pittsburg and Blue Valley school districts. His poetry has appeared in the *Kansas Quarterly, The Midwest Quarterly, The English Journal* and the *Laurel Review.* He is presently a co-editor of The *Little Balkans Review.* His books of poetry are *The Last Hippie of Camp 50* (Woodley Press 1988) and a chapbook, *Slow Stirring Spoon* (High/Coo Press 1981). Another book is forthcoming from Woodley.

Linda Rodriguez has published two books of poetry, *Skin Hunger* (Potpourri Publications) and *Heart's Migration* (Tia Chucha Press). Recipient of the 2009 Elvira Cordero Cisneros Award from the Macondo Foundation and the 2009 Midwest Voices and Visions Award from the Alliance of Artists Communities and the Joyce Foundation, she is vice-president of the Latino Writers Collective, founder of the Kansas City Women Writers Series, and a founding board member of The Writers Place. Rodriguez has published poetry and fiction in numerous journals and anthologies, as well as a cookbook, *The "I Don't Know How to Cook" Book: Mexican*. She is currently working on a book of poetry based on teachings from her Cherokee grandmother.

Ralph Salisbury, Professor Emeritus-University of Oregon, is the author of ten poetry books and three books of short fiction. Among his titles are: *Light From a Bullet Hole: Poems New and Selected; Blind Pumper at the Well; Rainbows of Stone; Going to the Water: Poems of a Cherokee Heritage; The Indian Who Bombed Berlin; The Last Rattlesnake Throw;* and *One Indian and Two Chiefs*. Among his awards are a Rockefeller Foundation Residency at Bellagio, Italy; the Chapelbrook Award; the Northwest Poetry Award; and Fulbright professorships. For six years the editor-in-chief of *Northwest Review*, Salisbury also has edited *A Nation Within*, an anthology of Native American writing (Outriggers Press, New Zealand), and is Guest-Editor of *Yellow Medicine Review* (2010).

William Sheldon received an M.F.A. at Wichita State University (Creative Writing 2006); M.A. and B.S. in English, Emporia State University English (1986, 1984); and A.A. Dodge City Community College (1982). He has worked as a carpenter's assistant, stage coach driver, bus station attendant, and journalist; for the last 17 years he has taught at Hutchinson Community College. His books are *Retrieving Old Bones* (Woodley 2002, Kansas City Star Noteworthy Book) and *Into Distant Grass* (chapbook *Midwest Quarterly*, 2008). He received a Kansas Arts Commission fellowship.

Kim Stafford is a writer and teacher living in Portland, Oregon. He is the founding director of the Northwest Writing Institute, a zone for exploratory writing at Lewis & Clark College. His books include *Having Everything Right: Essays of Place* (Sasquatch Books), *The Muses Among Us: Eloquent Listening and Other Pleasures of the Writer's Craft* (U. Georgia Press), *A Thousand Friends of Rain: New & Selected Poems* (Carnegie Mellon University Press), and *Early Morning: Remembering My Father, William Stafford* (Graywolf Press).

Robert Stewart edits *New Letters* magazine, a 2008 National Magazine Award winner; *New Letters on the Air* radio series; and BkMk Press. He teaches poetry, nonfiction, and editing at the University of Missouri-Kansas City. Books include *Outside Language: Essays* (finalist in the PEN Center USA Awards 2004, winner of the Thorpe Menn Award); and *Plumbers* (poems).

Ingrid Wendt is the author of four books of poems, one chapbook, two anthologies, a teaching guide, numerous articles and reviews. Over 200 poems appear in journals, including: *Poetry, Poetry Northwest, Antioch Review, Northwest Review, Ms.,* and *No More Masks! An Anthology of 20th Century American Women Poets.* Wendt has taught at all educational levels, including the MFA program of Antioch University Los Angeles; at teacher-training institutes; and in public schools in Oregon, Washington, Utah, Illinois, Iowa, and overseas. Honors include the Oregon Book Award, Pushcart nominations, Editions Prize, Yellowglen Award, the Carolyn Kizer Award, an Oregon Literary Arts Fellowship, and the D.H. Lawrence Award.

Fred Whitehead, Ph.D., is co-editor of the anthology *Freethought on the American Frontier* and recently published *In Transit,* a suite of poems arising from his work as a bus driver in suburban Kansas City. Other editing projects are *Collected Poems* by Don Gordon (with introductory essay, University of Illinois Press 2004) and *Culture Wars: Opposing Viewpoints.* He has produced and directed films, including *John Brown in Kansas*, with the novelist Truman Nelson; and *A Commemoration of the 150th anniversary of John Brown's Raid on Harpers Ferry Held in Kansas City, Kansas, October 16, 2009.* He edited *Quivera,* a literary publication.

William Stafford (1914-1993) was born in Hutchinson, Kansas. As he grew up he also lived in Wichita, Liberal, Garden City, and El Dorado. He graduated from the University of Kansas with a B.A. (1937) and an M.A. in English (1946). He received a Ph.D. from the University of Iowa in 1954. He taught at Lewis and Clark College in Oregon from 1948 to 1980.

Stafford's second book of poems, *Traveling Through the Dark* (1962), won the National Book Award. In 1970, he was selected as the Consultant in Poetry to the Library of Congress (a position currently known as the Poet Laureate). Other honors include a Guggenheim Fellowship, a Shelley Memorial Award, the Award in Literature by the America Academy and Institute of Arts and Letters, Poet Laureate of Oregon, and a Western States Lifetime Achievement Award in Poetry. He published more than sixty-five volumes of poetry and prose by the end of his life.

CPSIA information can be obtained at www.ICGtesting.com

263225BV00003B/209/P

9 780981 733463